16/8/2016 24

D1535608

AUSTIN CITY LIMITS

AUSTIN CITY LIMITS

A History

Tracey E. W. Laird

OXFORD
UNIVERSITY PRESS

OXFORD
UNIVERSITY PRESS

Oxford University Press is a department of the University of Oxford.
It furthers the University's objective of excellence in research
and education by publishing worldwide.

Oxford   New York

Auckland   Cape Town   Dar es Salaam   Hong Kong   Karachi
Kuala Lumpur   Madrid   Melbourne   Mexico City   Nairobi
New Delhi   Shanghai   Taipei   Toronto

With offices in

Argentina   Austria   Brazil   Chile   Czech Republic   France   Greece
Guatemala   Hungary   Italy   Japan   Poland   Portugal   Singapore
South Korea   Switzerland   Thailand   Turkey   Ukraine   Vietnam

Oxford is a registered trademark of Oxford University Press
in the UK and certain other countries.

Published in the United States of America by
Oxford University Press
198 Madison Avenue, New York, NY 10016

Library of Congress Cataloging-in-Publication Data

Laird, Tracey E. W.
Austin city limits : a history / Tracey E. W. Laird.
pages cm
Includes bibliographical references and index.
ISBN 978–0–19–981241–7 (hardback : alk. paper)
1. Austin city limits (Television program)   2. Country music—History and
criticism.   I. Title.
ML3524.L28 2014
791.45′72—dc23

1 3 5 7 9 8 6 4 2
Printed in the United States of America
on acid-free paper

for Zoey and Henry—you got this!

CONTENTS

AUSTIN CITY LIMITS

INTRODUCTION

Five years after it began, the *Austin City Limits* Music Festival had the kinks worked out. An underground watering system kept the grass alive in Zilker Park in 2006 and prevented the plague-grade dust storm that choked festival goers the previous year. In a streamlined achievement of human engineering, a city bus fleet transported 60,000–70,000 visitors per day from parking lots in downtown Austin to the festival site. A shade tent and free watering holes offset the chance for collective heatstroke in the 95-plus-degree temperature of a Texas September weekend.

That year the sheer variety of musical acts struck me more than anything. Rock artists like Tom Petty and the Heartbreakers and Van Morrison whose appeal crossed generations performed as headliners. People alternately danced or stood rapt at the performance by Matisyahu, the Hasidic singing-rapper whose music blends Jamaican dub and dancehall with forthright lyrics about the power of spiritual forces in a troubled world. Gnarls Barkley brought their wacky eclecticism from Atlanta to Austin—with four string players, three backup singers, horns, and the core rhythm section all decked out in white lab coats and big black glasses, blasting an instrumental version of that quintessence of the 1980s, Thomas Dolby's "She Blinded Me With Science." Los

Figure 0.1 Matisyahu performing at the 2006 *ACL* Music Festival

Figure 0.2 People alternately danced or stood rapt at the performance by Matisyahu in 2006

Amigos Invisibles, famous in their native Venezuela before moving to New York, lit up the Wachovia tent by mixing Latin rhythms with a disco house sound. Smaller tents came to life via performances by a variety of regionally known country pickers, zydeco rockers, and gospel harmonizers while Los Lobos ignited the big stage with their distinctive L.A. Chicano rock. The New Orleans–based jam band Galactic performed a funky instrumental set. Later, another group of musicians from New Orleans, brought together by Hurricane Katrina and including George Porter Jr. and other legends, performed together as the New Orleans Social Club. And then there was the neo-reggae of Damian Marley, youngest of the many musically gifted sons of the legendary Bob Marley.

Of all the musical performances over that September 2006 weekend, Saturday's headliner seemed a fitting symbol for the unique

Figure 0.3 Gnarls Barkley decked out in lab coats for Thomas Dolby's "She Blinded Me With Science"

Figure 0.4 Buckwheat Zydeco at the 2006 *ACL* Music Festival; at one point he said, "I'm not trying to mess in anyone's business, but every now and then I'm going to ask how y'all are doin'."

character of the *Austin City Limits* Music Festival, better known as *ACL*. Willie Nelson played to a tremendous crowd, several football fields deep. From where I stood on the grass near one guy from New Jersey and another guy from Alaska, we strained even to see Willie's image projected on the large screens to either side of the stage. Some technical problems made Willie's sister, Bobbie, hard to hear at the piano and Willie's vocal mike occasionally cut out. Still, most of the crowd seemed content simply to be in Willie's presence. Here was an icon of American music, of Austin musical identity, and a living symbol of the meaning and history of the town's most well-known musical institution, *Austin City Limits*. When Willie launched into "Whiskey River," the song with which he customarily begins a live performance, a three-decades-wide musical circle closed.

Willie Nelson had performed that same song on the television pilot for *Austin City Limits* 32 or so years earlier, in 1974, at the studio for station KLRU (then KLRN), on the University of Texas campus. Were astrologers on hand they might have declared that 2006 night a Saturn Return, referring to the time when Saturn passes back through the same precise position it occupied at the moment of an individual's birth. Perhaps Saturn circled back to where it was when *Austin City Limits* first broadcast. Other metaphors come to mind as well. Willie Nelson's 2006 performance brought the downbeat that followed the gradual, building lead-in, or the chapter end when all the plot threads fell into place. The point is that Willie Nelson's performance at the festival intersected two, or perhaps three, overlapping historical trajectories: that of Austin music, or, to be more precise, of Austin as a musical city,

Figure 0.5 Willie's image projected on the large screens to either side of the stage, 2006 *ACL* Music Festival

and that of *Austin City Limits,* the PBS showcase upon whose reputation the festival sprang forth.

A strain of continuity links recent years of *Austin City Limits*
with the show's looser, more freewheeling early days. Its eclectic bookings maintain a careful balance between innovation
and connection with the past. In the case of the 2006 festival,
cutting-edge, hard-to-pin-down performers appeared alongside
an archetypal Texas singer-songwriter like Jimmie Dale Gilmore.
Texas luminary Guy Clark was there and moved the entire tent to
sing along with him. Younger Austin acts appeared, carrying on a
variety of traditions—the South Austin Jug Band, Iron and Wine,
Explosions in the Sky, to name a few. To juxtapose Los Lonely Boys
and Damian Marley is to create a gestalt for all the times when,
over the course of a long history, regional identity pulled against
national relevance; musical artistry bucked against the labels that
aimed to bring it into line; and art met commerce and negotiated
peaceful terms on *Austin City Limits.*

The history of *Austin City Limits* points to the ways musical
genre shifted in the United States from the mid-1970s to the present, as well as to ways people can experience music on television or
at a festival as simultaneously live and mediated. The *Austin City
Limits* story is one in which a scene, with particular parameters
of time and place, gave way to an institution; over the years that
institution took on the force of an idea that straddles multiple venues, media, and musical expressions. It is a peculiar and local story
of how a small staff—producer, director, sound engineer, camera
operators, photographer, lighting director—come together to
shape an exceptional artistic vision. At the same time, it is a big
story that sheds light on the process of finding musical meaning
in late-twentieth-century and early twenty-first-century popular
culture.

Figure 0.6 Guy Clark performs at the 2006 *ACL* Music Festival

At times my approach to the *ACL* story stays more "on the ground" to talk about the people and places anchoring *Austin City Limits*. At other times I take a perspective more from "up in the air" to consider aspects of *Austin City Limits* as a media phenomenon and a powerful idea in relation to television in general, and PBS more specifically, and in relation to its home city. *Austin City Limits* airs outstanding performances, and *Austin City Limits* shapes musical meaning and aesthetic experiences far outside the bounds of its hour-long TV program.

Chapter 1 sets up the pilot as the moment when Willie Nelson became the focal point—the mouthpiece—for the megaphone role *Austin City Limits* played during its first season, blasting the local scene to PBS stations across the country. Over time the show became less like a megaphone and more like a satellite, absorbing musical signals from all over and beaming them outward in new directions. In hindsight, Nelson embodied all that came to define *Austin City Limits*: as seamlessly as he moved from honky-tonking to Hoagy Carmichael, *Austin City Limits* stitched together season after season of artists whose work transcended labels.

Chapter 2 frames the first five seasons as the period when essential elements for the show's success fell into place. Following the first year, *Austin City Limits* continually redefined itself in relation to both its local Austin context and its larger national television audience. Artist lineups offer one way to gauge the changes. So do press releases, programming proposals, and other in-house materials through which *Austin City Limits* articulated its shifting vision. In seasons 4 and 5, *Austin City Limits* caught its stride, establishing a national presence for itself and its home city and settling into the flexible groove that sustained the show during the decades to follow.

Chapter 3 breaks from the chronology of the show itself to delve into the idiosyncratic story of the crew, remarkable for its stability and its shared artistic vision. Terry Lickona, producer since Season 4, is the central figure steering *Austin City Limits* for over three decades, and part of the show's success clearly stems from Lickona's good taste. Other people contribute essential components as well. Among them, producer Jeff Peterson started with the show over 30 years ago, moving from audio supervisor into production; working with associate producers Leslie Nichols and Emily Joyce, he combines his creative instincts with the more technical or nuts-and-bolts aspects of producing a show. Director Gary Menotti began as a 19-year-old cable puller, gradually working through the ranks and developing a gift for live direction that often leaves his "rough cut" largely intact for the final airing. The camera operators deliver him images that capture the inimitable quality of musical performance. David Hough mixed sound for

Austin City Limits on the Nelson pilot. Walter Olden's lighting direction and Scott Newton's still photography create an immediately recognizable visual style. Taken as a whole, its distinct audiovisual signature communicates the vitality of live music on *Austin City Limits*. That style results from the individual and collective competence of the team putting the show together. From the stage manager to the camera crew, from the editors to the sound director, from the lighting crew to the director, no single person is responsible for the way things have come together every season for nearly 40 years now. Their combination of skill, instinct, and aesthetic vision turns out to be an extraordinary thing.

Chapter 4 picks up *Austin City Limits* history from the early 1980s to explore its growing and evolving reputation as it unfolds in parallel with that of its home city. At this era's beginning, *Austin City Limits* identified with "country" as a musical moniker, a term gradually replaced by the looser labels "Americana" or "roots." By the mid-1990s, even those came to seem too confining. During the same years of changing identity for *Austin City Limits*, Austin itself experienced a growing sense of wherewithal about the role of music in its civic culture and economy. It came into its own as the "live music capital of the world." The stories of Austin and *Austin City Limits* intertwine during the 1980s and 1990s so that people far and wide know both the city and the show as a special place for music.

Chapter 5 treats the twenty-fifth anniversary as a turning point for *Austin City Limits*. People working on the show came to realize its value as a musical institution within the larger US popular culture. Having evolved from local beginnings in progressive country to unbound notions like "originality," *Austin City Limits* began taking on extended life beyond the television program. The concept of a "media brand" signaled a transformation of thinking that was prompted by internal changes at KLRU, along with external pressures from the television industry in general and public broadcasting in particular. This brand-new thinking positioned the station to seek financial stability on the grounds of its trusted name and broader meaning. *Austin City Limits* had accrued a sense of cultural cachet or "cultural capital" for the way it communicates a strong regional identity (but avoids provinciality), and a sense of quality that is authentic, cutting-edge, or both. Around the turn of the just-passed century, media trends like the rise (or return) of more eclectic local radio stations, XM radio, iPods, and Internet tools like Pandora or Genius directly tapped more fluid notions of good or hip music, beyond genre, and in line with *Austin City Limits*.

Chapter 6 again steps out of the forward chronology to look at the program's live aesthetic, one of its most striking qualities, and a distinctive contribution to music on television from a long historical view. Its minimalist aesthetic of musical performance visually sets *Austin City Limits* apart from typical televised music that ranges from elaborate, now-classic videos to ongoing and ever-more ostentatious award shows like the Grammys or the Country Music Association Awards. Performers often leave the show impressed with the sense of spontaneity and immediacy they rarely experience in television. And audiences access unique insights into music-making that rarely come through the television screen.

Chapter 7 looks specifically at the significance of *Austin City Limits* in relationship to PBS. The ideals that built the public broadcasting system made way not only for the creation of *Austin City Limits*, but also for its sustenance through decades of development: from showcasing the progressive-country subculture, itself somewhat elusive, through times when the show's contents were difficult to pinpoint, and eventually to a time when its once-troublesome musical ambiguity became both asset and source of pride. The show's open attitude, "sense of discovery," or appreciation for "good music" are attributes directly contingent on the PBS system that frames it.[1] At the same time *Austin City Limits* helped shape the identity of PBS, which was still young when the show began and the Boston Pops stood out as adventurous music programming. In the end the show's meaning derives in part from its complex association with PBS, which bolsters *Austin City Limits* as a signpost for quality in an exponential world of musical options.

Chapter 8 returns to Austin, its Zilker Park, and the 75,000 people who, depending on the year, endure dust storms or slog through three-inch-deep mud fields to experience a festival weekend. For some the festival is a site of pilgrimage. In 2009, the year of the eighth annual *ACL* Music Fest, I flew from Atlanta next to a Pittsburgh couple who had attended every festival except the first. I rode the shuttle beside a fellow who had paid $160 (approximately double the normal price that year) on the street for a single-day Sunday ticket. Many people come to the festival at great effort and expense to confirm and enact their love of music. The sense of "being there" draws some festival goers for a particular act—for one Austin friend it was the Kings of Leon in 2009— and others from a more general confidence that even the artists unfamiliar to them must be worthwhile if they appear at *ACL*. The audience creates and sustains the feeling of vitality that defines the festival experience despite variables of comfort (a half-day deluge on Saturday) or sound quality (near-constant acoustic bleed from other stages). That vitality intertwines with Austin's identity as "live music capital" and of *Austin City Limits* as its defining cultural export. Factors both tangible and ineffable—Austin as both city and idea, and *Austin City Limits* as both television show and media brand—instill the *ACL* Music Festival with a unique range of potential meanings that hover somewhere between live and mediated experience.

Chapter 9 ponders the most recent development in *Austin City Limits* history, the 2011 opening of the new venue, known as *ACL* Live at the Moody Theater. *Austin City Limits* moved from its long-time studio on the University of Texas campus, and away from its parent station KLRU, into a downtown Austin development called Block 21, intended for mixed use in the modern urban way. The new space functions in two ways. Fifty or more days out of the year it functions as a television recording studio, still striving for an intimate feel yet capable of seating five times as many audience members as the former Studio 6A. When not used for recording, the space operates as a site for live music.

Figure 0.7 Still image from Willie Nelson's pilot performance on *Austin City Limits*

Undoubtedly this and future changes in the people, places, and media that constitute the meaning of *Austin City Limits* will continue to unfold. There is no way to know exactly if and how *Austin City Limits* will hold fast to its identity as a preeminent cultural force that connects audiences with music. But there is precedent for navigating a creative tension between a local, regionally grounded sense of authenticity and a wide-ranging hipness that speaks beyond Austin. Willie Nelson established the precedent on the pilot for *Austin City Limits* in 1975. In 2006 he reminded us that confirming a link between the place of Austin and the more free-roaming idea of "good music" is something *Austin City Limits* has done over and over again for decades.

At an intersection where places and sounds and people and images and words and ideas about music take on intangible meanings, there lies the musical phenomenon *Austin City Limits*.

[1]

A RHINOCEROS IN YOUR BATHTUB

In the pilot of *Austin City Limits*, Willie Nelson performs a set before a live audience seated in a 360-degree arrangement around the band. People sit on the floor, others in short risers, and some move about while the band plays, just as they might in a club—bobbing, jostling, clapping their hands in time with the music. Someone gets up, perhaps to grab a Lone Star, free beer being a prominent feature of any *Austin City Limits* taping. An audience member looks distractedly off in the distance, only to have his attention recaptured as Willie begins the second verse of "Good Hearted Woman." Mostly the camera focuses unobtrusively on the performers. Something that catches Willie's eye makes him chuckle midway through the first line. He smiles at someone in between phrases. The camera tracks the song: a close-up on the harmonica player's solo, then a piano break. With his eyes Willie cues the harmonica player that the more energetic second chorus is coming with the next downbeat. A key change in double time drives the song to an end and the applause erupts. While the style and look of *Austin City Limits* has changed during the nearly four decades since this pilot, the spirit of the show remains intact. The pilot communicates the feel of a live, small-venue performance, only a television screen away, and artfully makes that seem not very far at all.

Figure 1.1 Willie Nelson smiles at someone in between phrases of "Good Hearted Woman" in a still image from the pilot performance on *Austin City Limits*.

During the decade or so prior to 1974, a scene grew up in Austin around the clubs supporting live musicians and the energy generated from the local student population at the University of Texas.[1] Because of the commercial success and national notoriety of Willie Nelson, Jerry Jeff Walker, and Michael Martin Murphey, the 1974 local scene in Austin correlated with a country-rock hybrid sometimes labeled "redneck rock" or "hip hillbilly."[2] The same phenomenon had other names too. Steve Fromholz, a singer-songwriter associated with the Austin scene, suggested his own descriptive term for the long-haired, cowboy hat–wearing country-rocking crowd: "hickies," or people who are "almost a redneck and almost a freak."[3] Another name, the "cosmic cowboy movement," came from the title and first cut of a 1973 album by Michael Martin Murphey.[4]

Members of the scene self-consciously—at times, defiantly—
associated themselves with a particular version of Texas identity. Murphey's song is a case in point, beginning one verse with
a pointed reference to Texas beer: "Lone Star sippin' and skinny
dippin' and steel guitars and stars, Just as good as Hollywood and
them boogie-woogie bars...." Nostalgic in spirit and antimod-
ern in posture, the song draws on a tradition of Texas-centered
musical romanticism that dates back at least to 1910, when John
Lomax first published his collection *Cowboy Songs and Other
Frontier Ballads*. Lomax emphasized the authenticity of the music
he collected—a sense that these songs constituted a valuable treasure from the past, a rare find in a rapidly changing society.[5] Like
Appalachia, Texas enjoys a symbolic history as a kind of cultural
antidote to modernization: a mythic spot, a world apart from the
rest of the country. Scholars and writers like Lomax began a tradition carried on by the phonograph industry and other commercial
enterprises. They all cast Texas and its music as distinct from the
broader nation. Texas music was more authentic, more real, and
larger than life.[6]

The song's sound also typifies the 1970s Austin scene: instrumentation of country music (steel guitars, fiddles, and so on)
paired with smart, quirky, Texas- (or at least Western-) oriented
lyrics that were sometimes sentimental, sometimes irreverent,
sometimes satirical or tongue-in-cheek. Murphey later said he
intended his song to poke fun at what he saw as a trendy and
shallow marriage of disparate cultural impulses, but his words
stuck nevertheless. Tongue-in-cheek or not, the song draws
together various threads that made up the loose fabric of the
1970s Austin scene, a group of Texas singer-songwriters comfortable and familiar with country and rock, as well as older
blues styles.

The scene was inspired by the hippie movement and antagonistic to corporate commercialism. It longed for lost contact with nature and explored notions of freedom related to that perennial American fixation with the frontier West. The music invited audiences to listen to the stories or the poetry, or to sing along, to escape from the constraints of modern society, if only for a few minutes. Townes van Zandt might spin a tragic tale in a song like "Tecumseh Valley," while Jerry Jeff Walker mused about a gifted bootmaker named Charlie Dunn. Hondo Crouch talked his way through a lyrical meditation on a "Luckenbach Daybreak." Everyone joined in with Augie Meyers's rousing accordion-driven number "Down to Mexico." When it wasn't quirky and funny— "a supernatural country rockin' galoot," to quote another line of Murphey's song—it could be evocative, nostalgic, heartbreaking, vaguely yearning. The press and the music industry finally settled on the term "progressive country" to identify all that was happening in Austin from the late 1960s through the mid-1970s.

Several institutions arose in and around Austin to support and sustain the scene. Among them was the annual Kerrville Folk Festival. This event grew from earlier outdoor festivals and small venues dating back to the mid-1960s—including Austin's Zilker Park Summer Music Festival and the Chequered Flag folk music club—and, earlier, from a long tradition of honky-tonks and dance halls. Perhaps most deeply associated with the 1970s Austin scene was the Armadillo World Headquarters, a cavernous one-time armory converted to a live venue with its own staff artist who created posters for its events. While the Armadillo ultimately failed on financial terms, it came to be seen as the spiritual epicenter of Austin in the 1970s.

The Armadillo World Headquarters stood out as only the most famous of many clubs drawing musicians and audiences to the Texas capital. Nightspots like the Broken Spoke, Texas Opry House, Split Rail, and One Knite regularly featured live music. The Armadillo World Headquarters featured "progressive country" artists, as well as those playing blues, r&b, and others with styles difficult to pigeonhole. Crowds gathered to hear Freddie King perform "Hide Away" and play his blues guitar on one night. On another, they heard Waylon Jennings sing "Ain't No God in Mexico" and other hole-in-your-boot and bourbon-on-your-breath "outlaw country" songs. They paid $3.50 apiece for two shows in one night—1,500 people at each show—where Frank Zappa played "Theme from Burnt Weeny Sandwich" and other abstruse proto-art-prog jams. The Armadillo operators aimed to create a dual-purpose "cultural arts laboratory" and "beer garden of Eden," featuring everything from reggae to once-per-month ballet, with a crowd that included "blue-haired ladies dancing with bikers watching."[7] In the end the Armadillo never kept economic pace with its grandiose artistic vision and ideology. It closed in 1980, but remains iconic for a special musical era in Austin, a sacred spot that lives in the collective memory decades after the building was torn down.

Time magazine explained Austin with an analogy. In a story from its September 9, 1974 issue, the writer compared the Armadillo to San Francisco's Fillmore: as the Fillmore was to 1960s rock so the Armadillo was to "Austin's country-rock set."[8] The title of the article, "Groover's Paradise," referred to musical free spirit Doug Sahm, a San Antonio native. It noted that "more than 200 musicians, vocalists and songwriters" relocated to Austin over a span of two years or so, and 65 Austin-based bands enjoyed regular gigs. The writer described Armadillo audiences as "a curious amalgam of teenagers, aging hippie women in gingham, braless coeds, and booted goat ropers swigging Pearl beer and swinging

Stetsons in time to the music." *Record World* devoted a special section of their March 6, 1976 publication to this scene, characterized by writer David McGee as " 'a state of mind become reality,' which had its roots in the social upheaval of the '60s."[9]

In the meantime public television station KLRU (known at the time as KLRN) needed innovative programming. The Texas legislature had invested a heap of state money into the University of Texas Communications program. To justify the three-building complex dominating the intersection at 26th Street and Guadelupe, KLRN sought to expand its lineup with local productions. Bill Arhos gets credit for the station's best new idea. Arhos had first joined the station in 1961 as a graduate intern, and initially did production work on an experiment in educational television called the Texas Microwave Project. Over the years he worked his way up the ranks: producer, director, program manager, and then program director for the station. In 1986 he became the station's general manager and president. He retired in 2000. The closing credits for *Austin City Limits* included "Created by Bill Arhos" for years. (Six months after *ACL* Live at the Moody Theater opened in 2011 Arhos told me that he had "only been to the new venue once, and that a fundraiser, but they gave me another plaque.")[10] As Arhos recalled it, the inspiration for *Austin City Limits* came directly from the local scene. The show's first producer, Paul Bosner, envisioned it as a televised version of the Armadillo's simple magic: put a rug on the floor and have a concert.[11]

KRLN had already originated successful news-type broadcasts and bilingual children's shows, including one set in a mythical village called *Carrascolendas,* and a dramatic series for young viewers, *Sonrisas* (Smiles). Viewers appreciated these shows, but the station's board of directors wanted programs with stronger national appeal. They pointed to NOVA, the long-running science

Figure 1.2 Still image of the original set of *Austin City Limits*: put a rug on the floor and have a concert.

series out of WGBH in Boston, which was started in 1974 through a partnership with the British Broadcasting Corporation (BBC). Years later Arhos recalled the push for KLRN to create programs of NOVA-size stature. He sometimes had a hard time conveying to board members Austin's financial disparity with its Boston counterpart. Years later he recalled these exchanges: "We don't have any money and there's no infrastructure.... Yeah, we got a $6 million budget but Boston has a $100 million budget. They went to the BBC and studied their science programming for a year—they sent three people over there, and we can't send three people to, you know, Round Rock."[12]

A live music program would be relatively inexpensive to produce, particularly with the musical talent flocking to Austin at the time. Arhos applied for a grant from the Corporation for Public Broadcasting. With $13,000 the station shot two pilots, making it perhaps one of television history's greatest bargains. In fact, shoestring budgets would be normal operating conditions for at least the first 25 years of *Austin City Limits*. Those running the show could never be certain that the current season was not the last. Until the 2011 relocation to the Moody Theater, *Austin City Limits* still shot its widest overhead angles with a four-person crane camera used in 1937 on the set of *The Wizard of Oz*. They borrowed microphones from KUT, the public radio station downstairs in the same building, just to get through the pilot.[13] Today they own plenty of microphones. Still, while the budget grew from $165,000 for the entire first season to, for example, $585,000 for Season 10, the cost for 13 episodes remained approximately on par with a single episode of a commercial television series; while the 13 episodes that comprised Season 38 cost around $1.7 million,[14] the comparison remains

Figure 1.3 The big four-person crane camera, in motion during a double taping for *Austin City Limits* in 2007: Ghostland Observatory and The Decemberists.

reasonable. Another cost has remained constant throughout the show's history. Artists still receive union scale in 2014, just as Nelson did in 1974.

From the inception of *Austin City Limits*, the question loomed large: Will the program appeal to audiences? Music was and still is considered risky television fodder.[15] Commercial networks had tried live music shows before, such as *In Concert* on ABC and *Midnight Special* on NBC.[16] Chicago public television station WTTW began *Soundstage* the year before the *Austin City Limits* pilot. That show lasted until 1985; it was resuscitated in 2001, and remained in regular production until 2010. There had been local precedents for televising the Austin music scene as well. During the early 1970s, a fly-by-night, poorly advertised "mini-tour" called the "Armadillo Country Music Revue" culminated in a late 1973 live production featuring Willie Nelson, Michael Murphey, and the Armadillo's house band, Greezy Wheels.[17] It was simulcast on KLRN, which served both Austin and San Antonio at the time, and over radio stations in both cities. The Armadillo's spearhead Eddie Wilson helped produce the show, using KLRN equipment and expertise. He later emphasized to an interviewer: "We weren't talking about *country music,* we were talking about music from Armadillo country, which could be anything in the world."[18] Not one of these efforts gave good reason for imagining that *Austin City Limits* would eventually outlast every other live music TV program, public or commercial.

The precise origins of the show get a bit murky in hindsight. When asked about it by the local *Austin American-Statesman* newspaper in 1978, Arhos said that writers Jan Reid and Joe Gracey, the latter also an influential Austin radio character, first put forward the notion of a show built around the city's then-thriving progressive country music scene.[19] Reid wrote the 1974 book

The Improbable Rise of Redneck Rock about Austin music and would contribute regularly to *Texas Monthly* magazine over the next several decades, while also writing pieces for mainstream publications like *GQ* and *Esquire*. Gracey was deep into local musical life as a disc jockey and then program director at KOKE–FM, the radio station whose progressive country format won a *Billboard* Trendsetter award in 1974.[20]

Years later Arhos identified two others who'd been in on the ground floor: Paul Bosner and Bruce Scafe, the producer and director, respectively, of the first season, were the first to propose a music program.[21] Scafe and Arhos had worked together on the Armadillo Country Music Revue broadcast.[22] Bosner, who divided his time between Austin, where he worked, and Dallas, where his wife worked, spent many evenings taking in Austin bands. He lent Arhos a copy of Reid's book to help him catch up with what was happening in town. Arhos had the strong Public Broadcasting Service (PBS) connections. "By that time," he recalled, "I knew everyone in the system." So he took the idea to the man in charge of special projects at the Corporation for Public Broadcasting.[23] With a thin budget and long odds, Arhos faced a daunting challenge, but the vitality of Austin's indigenous music culture made his seminal work, and all the efforts that followed in his stead, much easier.

Looking back from this distance, *Austin City Limits* seemed to bubble up from the stream of musicians flowing into the city much as the local Barton Springs swimming hole emerges from the depths of the Edwards Aquifer. Progressive country filled every nook and cranny of Austin during the early 1970s. It was everywhere. Arhos later wisecracked that to think of highlighting this music for an Austin-based concert program was "like noticing a rhinoceros in your bathtub."[24]

To tape the pilot, they invited B. W. Stevenson, then riding a surge of popularity from his hit "My Maria." A *Time* magazine journalist had called Stevenson "the most commercially successful of the young Austin musicians" earlier that year. Despite his currency, however, publicity efforts had been so last-minute that only about 150 audience members were in the studio bleachers. That number looked skimpy from the camera's eye, so they scuttled the show. Stevenson later returned to tape another performance for that first season. Meanwhile they took a second shot at the pilot, this time with Willie Nelson because he was sure to draw a large local audience to the studio. In retrospect Nelson's appearance on the pilot broadcast for *Austin City Limits* was poetically prescient. His success inaugurated the show, and he remains intimately connected to it. Nearly four decades later, Willie Nelson, the city of Austin, and Austin's most famous cultural export, *Austin City Limits*, remain bedfellows. A bronze statue of Willie Nelson now stands in Austin on the corner of Second Street (now Willie Nelson Boulevard) and LaVaca Street, right in front of the Moody Theater, a testimony to this relationship.

In many ways Nelson's personal story is the story of a national love affair with progressive country. Two years before the pilot Willie Nelson already reigned as a local hero, celebrated for his much-publicized departure from the Nashville corporate country music world where executives embraced his songwriting pen at the same time they closed their doors to his singing voice. Born in 1933, Nelson grew up in central Texas, in the small town of Abbott, approximately 30 miles north of Waco. Some of his earliest musical experiences reflect the crossroads flavor of south central Texas. He gained his first performing experience, for example, as a 12-year-old guitarist in the Rejcek family polka band, playing Bohemian dance halls and beer joints.[25] Returning home amid the flowering of the local Austin scene, Willie Nelson sealed the association of this central Texas area with "progressive country" (sometimes overlapping with "outlaw country") and the image of the "hippie cowboy."

Nelson hosted his first Fourth of July picnic in 1973, drawing tens of thousands of people to a ranch in Dripping Springs, Texas.[26] In the words of music writer John T. Davis nine years later, the picnic "combined odors of marijuana and Old Spice," a remark that indicated the peaceful union of cowboy and hippie cultures.[27] These were the very same smells mingling together at the Armadillo. The picnics, however, drew far more media attention. Producers for the ABC television show *Midnight Special*, for instance, came to scout for musical acts. Nelson's picnics changed locations throughout the 1970s, moving from Dripping Springs to Liberty Hill, drawing bigger and bigger audiences from near and far. Some likened the event to a "Woodstock" for country music.[28] Yet performers at Nelson's picnics ranged much wider musically: from Kris Kristofferson and Rita Coolidge to Doug Sahm, from Leon Russell to the Pointer Sisters, who appeared in 1975.

By then Nelson epitomized "progressive country": a songwriter of extraordinary depth, a performer of extraordinary accessibility, a sockless hippie cowboy with a beat-up guitar and faded T-shirt. Even before *Austin City Limits*, Nelson reached a wide spectrum of listeners, breaking past margins of musical taste and category. Reflecting on the 1974 concept album *Phases and Stages*, produced by Jerry Wexler on Atlantic Records, *New York Times* critic Loraine Alterman, for example, wrote that Nelson's country music "can even move those of us who think we despise it." Along with his contemporary, Waylon Jennings, Nelson attracted followings at places Alterman never expected, like "Max's Kansas City here in New York or Los Angeles' Troubadour."[29]

Yet even with Captain Willie at the helm and all of Austin's cultural wind filling his sails, *Austin City Limits* embarked on a speculative voyage for television at the time of its 1975 pilot: an exploration that would test the appeal of a weekly, uninterrupted hour of live music in an intimate setting. At the time, televised live music most commonly occurred on variety shows hosted by big-name stars. There were no television channels devoted to music then, and most certainly not to country music. PBS was still young, only six years old in 1975, and perhaps the last place one might expect to find a guitar-wielding hippie cowboy. Still, it was worth putting it out there to see if a show drawn from Austin's music scene might capture broader interest.

One final detail remained. Before the program could air, it needed a title. Arhos bounced possibilities around with Bosner and Scafe, like "Hill Country Rain" or "River City Country," but nothing stuck. Then Arhos recalled the nice ring of *Macon County Line,* the title of an otherwise forgettable 1974 movie about a sheriff avenging his wife's murder. "Travis County Line" parroted this too obviously, but what about "Austin City Limits"? *Austin City Limits* tapped the contemporary buzz about the city's music scene, and might summon still deeper imaginings about Texas character.

While invoking both old and new Texas identity, *Austin City Limits* set up a potential paradox that might have proved an Achilles heel for the whole enterprise: possibly it was too local and yet not local enough, all at the same time. The name first seemed to work against the show's bid for national relevance. Why should TV viewers in Omaha or Syracuse or Fresno care about music hot in Austin, Texas? Then as the show's appeal became clear, the name gave ground for hometown criticism: Why don't more local acts appear on a national show with the city's name in its title? Or, in the words of one local newspaper writer 10 years later, "How much of Austin remains in *Austin City Limits*"?[30]

With the title set, now came the sell. Arhos recalled years later that the show more or less spoke for itself. He recounted for one *Dallas Morning News* writer how he mailed 22 copies of the Willie Nelson pilot to PBS colleagues with enough postage for them to mail it to another colleague, and, again, to send it on to yet one more. All 22 copies included a request that the cassettes be returned to the station. "I never got back one," said Arhos.[31]

The pilot aired in 1975, the same year Willie Nelson released *Red-Headed Stranger*. Critics swooned over the fresh voice the album brought to country music, long stultified by, to use one newspaper writer's words, "the time-tested country formula of basic vocal and instrumental tracks slathered with layers of schmaltzy strings."[32] From that perspective Nelson presented a sincere, stripped-down, more authentic country music, one that seemed familiar in the Austin scene. Outside Austin, country music more commonly evoked negative images, epitomized either as dangerous as the homicidal rapist hillbillies from 1972's *Deliverance*, or as simple as the cornball hayseeds hiding in fields on TV's *Hee-Haw*. Willie Nelson offered something different—a genuine songwriter who powerfully conveyed simplicity and sincerity, a poet for blue and white collar alike, whose reckoning of joy and pain, the sinful and the sacred, compelled listeners across the boundaries of genre set up by the label "country music."

Writing from Memphis, television critic Larry Williams reviewed the pilot and characterized Willie Nelson as "a cult hero, an accomplished artist who is content to stay home and reap the rewards of regional stardom."[33] He pondered Nelson's uncanny ability to communicate with audiences, and then placed him in distinguished musical company: "One could no more sit still listening to Willie Nelson than he could digging the far out sounds of a Bird, Prez or young Goodman, an early Beatles or a Woody Herman and the Third Herd." From within PBS circles, Bill Arhos sent a letter to fellow programming directors, urging their support for the program. He cited the success of the Nelson pilot in fund-raising, reporting more than $6,000 made by a California station in the break following the show. He went on to say, "A Florida station reports it as its second largest fundraiser between the Vienna Philharmonic and the Boston Pops." Near the end of the letter he writes, "We hope you will take this opportunity to give an unusual form of country music its first chance on PBS."[34]

Nelson's critical reception during this era set a tone for *Austin City Limits* as a dark-horse trailblazer. The year after *Red-Headed Stranger,* still one of the greatest concept albums of all time, came the release that named a country music subgenre, *The Outlaws,* with Waylon Jennings, Jessi Colter, and Tompall Glaser (1976). It would be the first-ever million-selling country album.[35] He followed this with the solo release *Stardust,* an album of Tin Pan Alley tunes. Nelson clearly scoffed at rigid musical categories. As he told the writer Bob St. John in 1975, "I hate music labels.... Labels put a bind on something, corner it and keep it from branching out."[36]

Meanwhile the pilot's timing coincided with Nelson's far-reaching critical buzz in 1975 and placed *Austin City Limits* right there with him in his uniquely hip corner of the musical universe. Nelson was grounded in the south central Texas region, yet expansive in musical taste. His music and his persona circulated outside the confines of any single genre. Too authentic to fit the slick formulas of Nashville, Nelson emerged as a one-man musical meeting ground in a pop culture landscape historically hell-bent on subdividing audiences by race, class, or region. Likewise, *Austin City Limits* established a show with a strong local identity and a strong sense of national relevance. The man and the show, not to mention their home base of Austin, entangled their destinies on October 17, 1974. This was the day on which Nelson taped the pilot, one ceremoniously named "Austin City Limits Day" by the mayor 35 years later.

[2]

"FREE FORM COUNTRY FOLK ROCK SCIENCE FICTION GOSPEL GUM EXISTENTIAL BLUEGRASS GUACAMOLE OPERA MUSIC"

By at least the mid-1990s, *Austin City Limits* creator and KLRU's then general manager Bill Arhos had taken to carrying a business card that read "It's free form country folk rock science fiction gospel gum existential bluegrass guacamole opera music."[1] To someone without a sense for Austin music history, Arhos's card would have reflected a characteristically tongue-in-cheek way to suggest that no music industry label fit *Austin City Limits*. This was, and happily remains, true. Yet for someone with deeper local knowledge, Arhos's card signified his nostalgia for the progressive country moment that begat *Austin City Limits*, building as it did on a phrase coined in 1969 by local musician Travis Holland and expanded by another progressive country luminary, Steve Fromholz.[2] It was that too, because, in the end, the words on Arhos's card contained multitudes, in the words of Walt Whitman, as did the television program it promoted.

Figure 2.1 Bill Arhos in 2007, at home with his *Austin City Limits* guitar, one of three made by Gibson, solid body with a cedar veneer using wood from the *Austin City Limits* stage. The neck includes an image of the skyline and an armadillo. Arhos has since loaned the guitar to Texas State University.

Austin itself rests at a crossroads of Hispanic, Anglo, Germanic, African American, and Cajun cultures. The conflict and cooperation among its Spanish-, German-, and English-speaking settlers shaped local culture and music. Black, brown, and white came together with a fluidity and familiarity that was oftentimes troubled but nevertheless unavoidable due to sheer proximity. That history forged a distinct character in central Texas, and a distinct local vibe. The lineup for *Austin City Limits* Season 1 communicated the city's particular cultural ambience to a national audience, bringing together music, symbols, words, and ideas that made sense in Austin and projecting them outward via what was at the time one of only four major television outlets.

During Season 1, only Willie Nelson enjoyed widespread name recognition, having won accolades from more than one *New York*

Times writer, gracing the cover of *Rolling Stone,* and earning the title "The King of Country Music" from *Newsweek* magazine.[3] Nearly everyone else required more exegesis. Thus *Austin City Limits* became the first effective stage for projecting Austin's musical identity to a broad audience. The program forwarded both the city's special ambiance and the unique aspects of Texas character as primary arguments for its own relevance. That first season began with the Western swing revival group Asleep at the Wheel and the survivors among Bob Wills's Original Texas Playboys, and ended with the "redneck rock" of folkie-turned-Austin-fixture Jerry Jeff Walker. In between, the show featured solo acts ranging from the poetic introspection of songwriter Townes Van Zandt to the extroversion of Doug Sahm or Marcia Ball, peppered from the east with the zydeco of Clifton Chenier and spiced from the south by the conjunto style of Flaco Jimenez.

One way *Austin City Limits* communicated the local scene came through its introductory segment each week. During Season 1, producer Paul Bosner ran the band members through a staged version of their sound check, right after the real one. He then used it as the audio to accompany each episode's two-minute-long opening visual sequence.[4] Along with this sound check, viewers saw a sequence of images that began with general scenes of Texas: isolated country roads and native Texas plant life, all very idyllic and pastoral in mood. With the appearance of a green-and-white "Austin City Limits" highway sign, the montage shifts to storefronts and signs for local nightspots like the Armadillo or Threadgill's or the Soap Creek Saloon. Austin insiders would know these places immediately, while audiences from outside the area would be drawn in via the travel motif. Taken as a whole, the opening images peg the show at once to deep-seated Texas mythos and to Austin's fresh scene.

Meanwhile, wordsmiths of various stripes set about explaining the show to its most important early audience: station managers and programming directors at PBS stations across the nation. Bill Arhos, then programming director, sent out a letter following the pilot, urging stations to choose the show during the Station Programming Cooperative (SPC) voting rounds.[5] Fueled by personal contacts and powers of persuasion, the SPC was a fairly recent and complicated experiment in decentralizing programming decisions for the Corporation for Public Broadcasting. Success within this system required support and buy-in from local public television stations. Thus early press releases tap every possible verbal resource to describe the program to stations far from the Texas capital and unfamiliar with its progressive country ethos. Selling the show meant selling Austin, since most early artists were largely unknown outside the region.

Somewhere between the pilot broadcast and the start of Season 1, a surviving press release marketed the content of *Austin City Limits* to these PBS programmers. It opens by reviewing the nomenclature for the "'Austin Renascence of Country Music,'...variously tagged as progressive country, cross country, redneck rock, cosmic country, underground country, and so on."[6] The text stresses the nature of the scene more than specific characteristics of the music: "the Austin progressive country scene provides a vigorous and thriving musical environment, nurturing not only itself, but other musical forms ranging from traditional/regional to contemporary jazz."

Progressive country comes across as less a musical sound than a mindset linked in a near-mystical, even "miraculous" way, to its location: "an anticommercial attitude, a local pride of community, and a strong sense of regionalism. Where else but in such a metaphorical oasis could the myth survive that the 'magic' sounds of

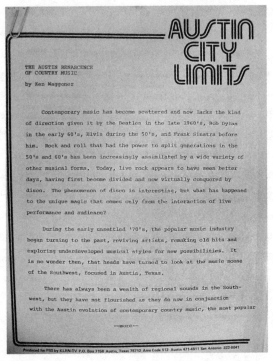

THE AUSTIN RENASCENCE
OF COUNTRY MUSIC

by Ken Waggoner

Contemporary music has become scattered and now lacks the kind
of direction given it by the Beatles in the late 1960's, Bob Dylan
in the early 60's, Elvis during the 50's, and Frank Sinatra before
him. Rock and roll that had the power to split generations in the
50's and 60's has been increasingly assimilated by a wide variety of
other musical forms. Today, live rock appears to have seen better
days, having first become divided and now virtually conquered by
disco. The phenomenon of disco is interesting, but what has happened
to the unique magic that comes only from the interaction of live
performance and audience?

During the early unsettled '70's, the popular music industry
began turning to the past, reviving artists, remaking old hits and
exploring underdeveloped musical styles for new possibilities. It
is no wonder then, that heads have turned to look at the music scene
of the Southwest, focused in Austin, Texas.

There has always been a wealth of regional sounds in the Southwest, but they have not flourished as they do now in conjunction
with the Austin evolution of contemporary country music, the most popular

—-more—-

Produced for PBS by KLRN-TV P.O. Box 7158 Austin, Texas 78712 Area Code 512 Austin 471-4811 San Antonio 222-8041

Figure 2.2 First page of a five-page early press release that positions *Austin City Limits* within the "Austin Renascence of Country Music." From Radio and Television, Folder 77, *Austin City Limits*, Southern Folklife Collection, The Wilson Library, University of North Carolina at Chapel Hill.

Austin's contemporary country music have the power to miraculously and simultaneously transform rednecks into 'cosmic cowboys' and hippies into 'redneck rockers'?" No one person better represented the musical sun storm transforming Austin by 1975 than Willie Nelson, evoked here for his stance against the "'formula' Nashville sound" and his support of regional artists. Press releases like this one reveal an aspect of the show's creative beginnings that time can buffer away from memory—the mindset of those who built the program and argued its broad appeal.

The people, often unattributed, writing press releases for *Austin City Limits* aimed to persuade their audience that this program mattered. On the one hand, these documents were ephemera, never intended for posterity, passing among a relative handful of people. At the same time, they articulate, episode by episode, the perspective of the team conceiving and producing the show. Anyone who writes words about music knows how difficult it must have been to wrap them neatly around the sounds happening in mid-1970s Austin and on Season 1 of *Austin City Limits*. In mainstream sources like *Time* and *Record World,* reporters grasped at conveying the living, breathing musical phenomenon abbreviated as progressive country to readers with no local experience to go on.

As folklorist Archie Green mused in 1981, tags like "progressive country" and "cosmic cowboy" "caught on because [they] helped us understand crossover music—music that meant not only tunes listed on folk, country, or rock charts, but also texts signifying deep social change."[7] For people into the mid-1970s Austin scene, these terms signified more of an attitude or mind frame than a specific or circumscribed musical sound. Frustrated in his efforts to reconcile music-making with music-talking, Green contended that music lovers need catchphrase nomenclature like "cosmic cowboy" "to describe those expressions which comment on the constant meeting of rural and urban, black and white, and innovative and conservative forces in America. A pluralistic society, with or without a transcendent national ethos, must find words to mark a people's travel across borders of class, ethnicity, and region."[8]

Press-release writers were far more pragmatic. They spun a kaleidoscope of references to musical styles, performers' names, regional history, events, and trends, hoping to strike at least one sympathetic chord with the reader. The press copy for Doug Sahm's first performance, aired as Season 1's fifth episode, makes a good starting point. It links Sahm to names or styles more likely familiar to a programmer in New York or Chicago or Little Rock. Evoking the Beatles, it describes Sahm's 1960s Sir Douglas Quintet as the first American band to employ "the English sound" with success, while his contemporary work mixes this "with his own brand of popular progressive country music (triplets, shuffles, rhythm & blues and rock & roll)."[9] The release mentions Bob Dylan and Dr. John among the personnel on Sahm's 1972 album, recorded in New York (but neglects to mention Jerry Wexler's production role). Sahm's repertoire includes T-Bone Walker blues numbers like "Papa Ain't Salty No More" and mainstream hits like "Wasted Days, Wasted Nights" by Freddy Fender, part of a "fun-filled rhythm & blues/rock & roll medley."

The press release asserts that no standard musical genre can account for Doug Sahm's music, which brings together wide-ranging resources but remains locally grounded. Sahm's childhood experiences in country music, "singing and playing the guitar, steel guitar, fiddle and mandolin for over six years" led to his forming a blues band in junior high and then "introducing San Antonio to the revolution of rock & roll during high school." After many accomplishments, the "Texas Tornado" returned to his home state where he is "one of the most talented and versatile musicians of the Austin progressive music scene."

These documents emphasize Texas identity, and Texas grounded the show within in a physical, geographic location. At the same time it provided a cerebral reference point for music that simultaneously alluded to "country" while exploding its perceived boundaries. This concept has legs. Texas distinction has been floated as an idea in scholarship at least since John Lomax wrote about *Cowboy Songs,* and in the marketing world at least since the early days of the phonograph industry.[10] Texas created enough conceptual room for the blurred stylistic edges that locals understood to be progressive country. For example, materials promoting Season 1's second episode hammer hard on the way Rusty Wier typifies Texas:

> Though he does not restrict himself to country music per se, Rusty Wier is as thoroughly Texas as his custom-made boots and beaver hat.... Drawing on the wide variety of music available in the Austin area, Wier and his band fuse their natural country instincts with rock, blues, and some Latin rhythms into original compositions like "Jeremiah Black,"...[other tunes named] which Rusty delivers while he banters with the studio audience in a frank and candid style that is characteristic of Texas.[11]

Texas further framed *Austin City Limits* as a place—a geographic focal point—where innovation meets tradition. Season 1's first episode, for example, paid tribute to the recently departed "King of Western Swing," Bob Wills, by featuring past members of his Texas Playboys alongside the more contemporary Western-swing revival group Asleep at the Wheel. Texas musicians like Bob Wills absorbed a variety of musical sounds and used them to create fresh traditions. Younger musicians like Ray Benson and other Asleep at the Wheel members migrated to Texas, valuing the authenticity and integrity of its traditions and carrying that history forward.

Like the Sahm example, the press writers for the episode also entwine references to wide-ranging genres, other artists, and song titles to convey its eclectic spirit. Bob Wills was born in Texas, "the son and grandson of championship fiddlers," but pioneered his own style by incorporating "virtually all of the popular styles of the day

Figure 2.3 Still image from Rusty Wier's second performance on *Austin City Limits*.

(big band, ragtime, dixieland and New Orleans jazz) into a musical form which, until that time, had been considered stable in its rural roots." Wills "pushed traditional instrumentation to its limits," using drums and horns in country music at a time when neither was common. His band's popularity rivaled that of Tommy Dorsey and Benny Goodman, associations that might not occur to the unfamiliar viewer watching these former Texas Playboys: eight fairly sedate, older men in coordinated cowboy hats and dress, fiddler Jesse Ashlock smoking on stage while he bows his instrument. Asleep at the Wheel, for their part, recouped lost tradition when their version of Wills's "Take Me Back to Tulsa" "uncovered a potent and basically untapped market." Their relocation to Texas is key to their story. Band members moved from "their Eastern city-homes to West Virginia," then San Francisco, and finally to Austin, where the group settled, expanded its membership, and "became recognized as the primary progenitors of western swing in the Bob Wills tradition."

This same theme of tradition and innovation drives the description of the fourth episode, but with a different regional twist. It features the border conjunto style of accordion player Flaco Jimenez. His father Santiago Jimenez, also a well-known musician, first blended "Mexican folk music such as the corrido (ballad)" with "danceable music based primarily on the Bohemian polka, imported to central Texas by early German, Czech, and Polish settlers. Reflecting much of the rich musical heritage of the Southwest, Flaco performs a unique mix of *conjunto*, country and western, Tex-Mex and Cajun music." Jimenez's performance of "La Cumbia" adds "Cuban and Caribbean rhythms" to the mix. He traverses broad regional musical traditions with a medley that "begins with 'Viva Seguin' and ends with 'Rancho Grande'... [and] also includes 'Turkey in the Straw' and 'San Antonio Rose,'" and he also does mainstream country music hits like "Pass Me By," a song made popular by Johnny Rodriguez.

When guitarist and singer Ry Cooder joins Jimenez on stage for "'He'll Have to Go,' all-time bestseller of the late Jim Reeves, a South Texas artist," the description turns to another element of Texas distinction: its friendly nature. Positive vibes and musical reciprocity come across as a matter of course in Austin. Musicians from different ethnic backgrounds exchange musical ideas in an atmosphere of shared appreciation:

> Ry is welcomed to the stage with handshakes by Flaco and Hugo Gonzales, bajo sexto guitarist in the band. The relationship of these great performers is one of mutual respect; Ry's interest in conjunto dates back some time. He appears on this show as Flaco's guest, following Flaco's recent visit to Los Angeles at Ry's request, to record some cuts for a new Ry Cooder album.[12]

Within the general framework of Texas, Austin stood out as epicenter for all good things the state represented. Taken collectively, Season 1 press releases weave together bits and pieces of Texas identity, Austin hipness, progressive country romanticism, Armadillo-hippie-cowboy-folk-Lone-Star-spirit into an early identity for *Austin City Limits,* a pretty full picture of what made its late-1960s-to-mid-1970s scene so special. Austin frames the appearance even for the two-out-of-nineteen Season 1 acts from outside the scene. For example, Creole accordion master Clifton Chenier and His Red Hot Louisiana Band are "musically at home in the Austin area." Paired in the third episode with Texas singer-songwriter Townes Van Zandt, the two acts share a "traditional folk music background." (The other outside-Austin act that first year was the Charlie Daniels Band.)

Austin City Limits staked its claim on public television by conveying a city of musical vitality framed under the broad auspices of progressive country. Its producers sealed this association when, in Season 2, they replaced the sound check with a theme song written by renowned local performer Gary P. Nunn. "London Homesick Blues" arguably stands out as progressive country's quintessential song.[13] A paean to the state, the chorus celebrated the program's Texas roots and the Austin music that sparked it. It gives a shout-out to the Armadillo and to two prominent Texas towns as it proclaims love for country music. Other more polished recordings of the song existed, including a well-known version by Jerry Jeff Walker, but Nunn and the Lost Gonzo Band's live cut captured the music's Texas honky-tonk roots and the raucous nature of Austin clubs. It sounds participatory, in the way a drunken sing-along is participatory. In short, when Nunn sang "London Homesick Blues," he sang the Austin progressive country scene.

At the same time Season 2 added Nunn's progressive country anthem, its programming reflected two competing demands: sustaining the show's roots in the local Austin scene, and sustaining the national audience and critical reputation successfully established on the strength of that scene. As a result, Season 2 featured Austin-based acts for just over half its performances. These included Texas singer-songwriters Willis Alan Ramsey and Steve Fromholz, as well as Clarence "Gatemouth" Brown, often labeled a bluesman although he referred to his own work as "American Music, Texas Style."[14] Acts from outside Austin included Earl Scruggs, Tracy Nelson, the Amazing Rhythm Aces, and Larry Gatlin.

From the documents left behind, *Austin City Limits* people obviously wrestled with the balance. In a proposal document for an upcoming SPC voting round, Arhos fleshes out its less-than-intuitive categories for booking Season 2. Still referring to it as a "progressive country music performance series," Arhos explains, "We've developed a content formula which cross sections the talent in a way we feel is both very entertaining and meaningful.

Artists/Writers—Guy Clark, Alex Harvey, Tracey [*sic*] Nelson, Larry Gatlin

Regional Popularity—Delbert McClinton, Willis Alan Ramsey, Gatemouth Brown, Denim

National Popularity—Jimmy Buffett, Amazing Rhythm Aces, Nitty Gritty, Firefall

Old Line—Earl Scruggs Revue (tentatively Chet Atkins and John Loudermilk)

Class By Itself—(Red Headed Stranger)[15]

Arhos communicated a wide-open spirit for *Austin City Limits*. In the end, Atkins and Loudermilk did not appear that year due to budget woes that sliced the anticipated 13 episodes down to 10. Nevertheless, *Austin City Limits* worked.

Popular and critical attention poured in from both within and outside the region. The Texas Association of Broadcasters gave *Austin City Limits* an award for cultural programming. The Country Music Association acquired a copy of the first season's historic Texas Playboys reunion for their Nashville archives. *Austin City Limits* won the *Playboy* magazine poll for "best musical program of the year" in 1977, along with "two certificates of merit from the 1977 Chicago Film Festival." One newspaper reported "talk of syndication with England and Australia."[16] PBS stations quickly picked it up; by 1978, the *Austin American-Statesman* reported that 216 out of 277 PBS stations in the United States carried the show.[17]

The early critical cachet of *Austin City Limits* reached as far as the Spring Festival at the American Center in Paris. There, a Season 2 episode featuring the Earl Scruggs Revue appeared among media presentations documenting all-things-American. Other topics included Georgia O'Keefe, Benny Goodman, childbirth, and the Junior Prom as experienced by a 1940s adolescent living in a steel town. The Festival also featured workshops with avant-garde dancer and choreographer Merce Cunningham and his frequent cutting-edge collaborator, composer John Cage. Bill Arhos saved a memo from one of the Festival's organizers, Barbara Van Dyke, who worked with the New York–based International Film Seminars. She indicated that the event had generated interest in *Austin City Limits* from French television broadcasters and suggested the show for possible inclusion for the 1979 second annual INPUT (INternational PUblic Television screening) conference, a gathering for TV programmers to exchange ideas and programs that continues to this day.[18]

Yet Austin and *Austin City Limits* were not fixed entities. Neither the term "progressive country" nor the scene it referenced remained stable. Progressive country had suggested a free and distinctly Austin mix of blues, rock, rhythm and blues, bluegrass, and country. If "progressive country" and related terms like "cosmic cowboy" once expressed more a state of mind than a specific range of musical sounds, their meaning gradually constricted. Progressive country pointed eventually toward a more focused intersection of country and rock, lightly touched by the blues, a Texas drawl, and an attitude of fun-loving defiance.[19] A handful of talented singer-songwriters, either emerging from or drawn to Texas, particularly Austin, during a circumscribed era of the 1970s, exemplified this sound. These artists and their music changed over time and, at some point, "progressive country" no longer resonated as it once had. It had completed its cycle of vitality and usefulness to distinguish Austin's contemporary scene and consequently fell out of circulation.

In other words, around the same time "London Homesick Blues" raised a Lone Star longneck during the opening credits on *Austin City Limits*, the scene and style it celebrated were on the wane. Austin college students hung up their cowboy hats and kicked off their Charlie Dunn boots to go hear more rock and punk and blues acts appearing in local venues.[20] These local changes seemed like handwriting on the wall to some early staffers, who likely figured the show had run its course. Producer Paul Bosner left after the first season, to be replaced by a different producer for each of the two seasons to follow.[21] Director Bruce Scafe departed after Season 2, reluctantly leaving public television for a higher-paying position in the Department of Human Services.[22]

The next two seasons were nerve-racking for some of the crew. The temperamental style of Season 3's director raised tensions on the set.[23] Sound engineer David Hough recalls overhearing it through his headphones. "The camera crew had a problem following his directions. When we had an open track I would record the headsets. And there was this amazing yelling."[24]

In terms of programming, Season 3 presented roughly equal numbers of Austin-based and national acts. That year includes, for example, more mainstream country artists like Merle Haggard and Chet Atkins. It also features well-known but slightly out-of-center country acts like Johnny Rodriguez and Michael Murphey (a one-time central figure for Austin progressive country), and others still harder to pin down like fiddler Vassar Clements, John Hartford, and singer-songwriters Steve Goodman and John Prine. An appreciation for the origins of more modern sounds, one of progressive country's appealing features, comes through in episodes devoted to guitar masters Doc Watson and Gatemouth Brown. A return to musical roots and to the first season comes through in separate shows for Bob Wills's Original Texas Playboys and Asleep at the Wheel. Other local figures include the Lost Gonzo Band and Bobby Bridger. In this season, when the act was of national stature, the artist tended toward country; when the act was local, the net was cast more broadly.

Austin City Limits as a practical television operation gradually caught its groove beginning in Season 4. Most significantly, Terry Lickona moved into the producer's role. Starting out as a volunteer production assistant, he stepped in at the point when Bill Arhos channeled his energies fully into his station-programming responsibilities. In fundamental ways, Lickona remains the heart and artistic guiding force of the show to this day, booking the acts and ultimately bearing

Figure 2.4 Photo of Terry Lickona (left) with the author.

responsibility for how it all comes together. Lickona is the "voice of *Austin City Limits*" in more ways than one. A former radio man, his voiceover introduces the artists each week. He has also spoken about the show most often and most publicly over the decades. Lickona's eclectic musical taste came through clearly during his first year as producer.

For Season 4 (1979), Lickona booked a motley lineup that included Tom Waits, Taj Mahal, Leon Redbone, the Neville Brothers, Marcia Ball, Lightnin' Hopkins, Little Joe y La Familia, Tom T. Hall, Esteban Jordan, Delbert McClinton, Bobby Bare, and Hoyt Axton, along with return visits from Clifton Chenier, Alvin Crow, and Steve Fromholz. From a programming point of view, *Austin City Limits* would venture so widely again only during the new century. At the time, the season confounded genre categories. That did not keep *Austin City Limits* people from trying to explain. Lickona told a journalist around the time that he looked for performers "with roots in country music or a certain earthiness that you could call country. It's difficult to put into words, but there is an honesty and an earthiness I identify with what real country should be."[25] *Austin City Limits* programming never did fall readily into a neat and tidy relationship with the vocabulary available to describe it.

Meanwhile, one piece had yet to fall into place. Season 4 saw a director shuttled in from New York, who completed editing for the entire season in seven days using a CMX video editing system in Nashville. Though common practice in television, both the level of tension and the marathon, long-distance sessions felt out of sync with the spirit in which *Austin City Limits* began. Thus, Hough's channel for the headsets, tuned to the back-and-forth between director and cameras, measured a second major shift in the fifth season when Allen Muir stepped into the director's post. He worked alongside his technical director, Gary Menotti, who started as a cable puller at KLRN and would eventually direct the show himself for decades. Under Muir, something fell into place, difficult to pin down. It had to do with the loose and flexible mindset that characterizes *Austin City Limits*. From Hough's perspective, the shift was palpable—or, at least, audible:

> The headset chatter then suddenly became very light because … there was no stress. They were very competent and they were laughing. The camera operators and the direction just got to this level of humor where everybody relaxed and, by then, the camera crew was a well-oiled machine and the director just had to give them a little bit of direction, and the camera guys were a little more creative in their pans and shuffles, and it was great.[26]

Since that time the equipment has changed more than the core crew. Menotti took over direction late in Season 7 (1982), applying the techniques he had absorbed from Muir's mentorship and bringing his own vision. As Hough summed it up, "Most of the time it's pretty much the same crew. Folks are still relaxed and having a great time and it's still fun."

Had *Austin City Limits* petered out, following the naturally diminishing course of progressive country, it still would remain a memorable archive for a distinct regional subgenre. It did not happen that way. In fact, just as the doors to the Armadillo closed for good, *Austin City Limits* expanded its reach. A press release from November 1980 reported that stations airing the program had grown from 80 in 1975 to 260, or 90 percent of all public television stations.[27] Progressive country or not, *Austin City Limits* had a show to produce. It carried on for years, marking a 10-year anniversary and then a 15, 20, 25, and on into the twenty-first century. Forty years after it started, *Austin City Limits* today is a television program and much more than that, at once remarkably different from, and yet continuous with, its 1970s beginnings.

At least in spirit the story of *Austin City Limits* from these early years to the present makes a kind of continuous circle in which recent seasons connect to the earliest ones. Season 37 (2011–2012), for instance, presented performances ranging from quiet, acoustic folk to stadium rock-and-roll, with traditional New Orleans jazz heritage acts, straight-ahead Country Music Award winners, R&B stylists, Europop sensations, and others filling the cracks in between: Mumford & Sons, Flogging Molly, Raphael Saadiq, Black Joe Lewis, Widespread Panic, The Decemberists, Gillian Welch, the Steve Miller Band, Preservation Hall Jazz Band, Randy Newman, Jeff Bridges, Miranda Lambert, Arcade Fire, The Head and the Heart, Gomez, Fleet Foxes, Joanna Newsom, Florence and the Machine, Lykke Li, Wilco, and Coldplay. Bill

Arhos had long since retired by then. Yet to sum up this lineup, perhaps no words better suffice than the ones he carried all the way back from 1969: perhaps this is how free form country folk rock science fiction gospel gum existential bluegrass guacamole opera music sounds after all.

[3]

CHANNELING THE DIVINE

Gary Menotti's direction of an *Austin City Limits* taping from the control room is a theatrical, ambidextrous performance often on par with the stage show. He stands before the monitors, hand poised to conduct like he's a maestro in the wings, ready to call the shots (quite literally here—he calls the camera shots). Chewbacca to his Han Solo is technical director Ed Fuentes, who sits at the board executing the calls as they unfold in real time. "Tight, Doug, tight," Gary tells Camera 1 operator Doug Robb to get him to tighten his frame on the guitar.

Up comes Gary's arm

"Ready Camera 1"

Gary's arm falls

"Go to Camera 1"

Up

"Ready 7"

Down

"7"

As Gary's arm comes down, Ed cuts from one shot to another. The muse seems just as present in the production room as on the stage of the Moody Theater. "Chris (Camera 5 operator), include the bass player to your right if you're going to get the drummer. Guitarist on 7 alone. Good job, 7. Standby 1—Dissolve 1."

Menotti prepares for this production/performance at the rehearsal earlier that day, with a stopwatch in one hand and a pencil in the other. Beginning at 0:00 for each song, he notes significant musical changes down one column: the singer comes in at 0:17, followed by a noteworthy guitar lick at 0:24. A bass solo begins at 1:15, followed by a drum break at 1:30. After rehearsal, he assigns the shots to one of seven cameras down another column. Somewhere between dinner time and show time, Menotti meets with the camera crew to talk through the night ahead. Musical performance is unpredictable, so the shot sheets only guide a series of calls that sometimes follow closely and sometimes do not.

Some performances require more improvisation than others. In the case of Damian Marley, for example, who recorded for Season 32 (2006–2007), there was very little rehearsal to plan around. During this kind of taping, something inexplicable—the muse, perhaps—fills any gaps in preparation. Menotti told me,

> There's an energy sometimes to shows that they can't help but be good.... It had a good energy when Damian came to me and said, "I don't really want to rehearse and it just kind of goes like this." And they did their thing and I just kind of followed, I kind of shot it from the hip.... You can't get the spontaneity in a rehearsal so they just leave it for that night to excite the audience.[1]

On a night like the Damian Marley taping, it becomes clear that the ability to convey compelling musical performance on *Austin City Limits* cannot be accounted for in the control room

Figure 3.1 Gary Menotti prepares for each performance during rehearsal, stopwatch in his hand.

alone. From there Menotti can only see what the camera operators show him, the images that feed through the camera lenses, minus the peripheral vision of people present in the studio during the performance. The camera operators are among those present, and, as one of them told me, "I always say that I've got the best seat in the house, and I do."[2] Within the parameters set by the director, the camera operators bring skill and intuition honed through longtime connections to the show, comfort with unpredictability, and deep musical sensibility.

Cameramen like Doug Robb and Robert Moorhead, for instance, worked for decades on *Austin City Limits*. Moorhead began as an intern in 1979.[3] Robb likewise stayed with the show for more than 30 years before moving on. He once reflected on his role in the production: "We are his eyes, and to a large extent his ears because even when he hears something, it's kind of up to us to be aware of what's going on at every moment. You know, he can't see what's happening in the audience so, if something good is happening that we would want to get on tape then it's up to us to shoot that and he can either say no thanks or great."[4] Years of interaction built trust and a synergy between the cameras on the set and the director in the control booth.

Walking from the control booth into the studio audience leads to another parallel performance, this one a strange, sideshow ballet. Two 600-pound pedestal cameras ("ped cams") flow within a very tight space in front of the stage. A camera operator will anticipate and frame a shot of a musician launching into a solo, only to suddenly swing 180 degrees to capture an audience reaction. The smooth, flowing, horizontal moves of the big cameras form part of the look of *Austin City Limits* on TV. The ped cams maneuver in tandem with two other cameras, also working close to the stage: at least one handheld unit stealthily operated by a camera operator in all-black camouflage, and a two-person smaller crane that moves in for distinctive angles from above or from below.

In the old Studio 6A, it took four people to operate the giant Wizard-of-Oz overhead crane that delivered yet another visual dimension from behind the audience. In Season 33, they replaced the old cameras with High Definition (HD) technology that sharpened the images and, most significantly, changed their frame to a letterbox format.[5] Moorhead reflected, "It's a much wider picture. That was a huge change because we went from almost a square 4 by 3 shooting ratio to this big 16 by 9." The result is "much more cinematic. It gives you a lot more stuff to play with aesthetically."[6]

The camerawork connects to the music. Both music and television cameras move, and the motion of the former directs the motion of the latter. Robb, himself a musician like many *Austin*

City Limits staffers, explained how he conceives their relationship, a perspective informed by his experience as a drummer in bands since the age of fifteen: "Everything is cut with the timing of the music, you know, in 4/4 time or 2/4 time or three-quarter time.... You always want to make the play of the motion fit the music."

When the Portland, Oregon–based band, The Decemberists, taped their first *Austin City Limits* in July 2007, Robb heard their music for the first time as he practiced camera shots at rehearsal. His first musical impressions were "kind of like sea chanteys meet rock-and-roll and folk" with lead singer Colin Meloy's sharp tenor voice "like James Galway does Procol Harum." With the camera rolling, he let the musical cues coordinate his moves with the ped cam. He recalled after the show: "You saw that I was doing a dolly

Figure 3.2 Camera operator Doug Robb practices shots during a rehearsal for The Decemberists in 2007; band member Jenny Conlee is visible to the right.

move into the singer, and then I would zoom in, zoom in until I got to a close-up. So I might have started out on him head-to-foot, and then ended up zooming in all the way—and that could be two lines of a song before we get to the chorus." Robb speaks of his role like a musician talks about playing in an ensemble:

> And then Gary [Menotti] cuts to the next camera that's got the main singer and two other people who are singing with him generally on the chorus.... There's an integration of movement with the music that basically underscores the energy of the music. You can really support the energy. And when it really comes together—it's magical.

The synergy between cameras and director extends to a larger web of people, all simultaneously focused on transmitting the energy of live performance. The lighting director, for example, significantly fashions the signature look of *Austin City Limits*—one reason why a TV channel surfer recognizes an episode of *Austin City Limits* even with the sound muted. Like the camera team, the lighting staff brings perspective earned over many years' experience with the show. Walter Olden officially replaced longtime lighting director Bob Selby when he retired in 2006, but Olden had worked closely with Selby since the 1980s. He began contracting for *Austin City Limits* in 1982, as the second driver for the big crane camera crew, working on the set and the risers, and then moved into the role of lighting technician. While taking on increasing responsibility with the show, he also started his own Olden Lighting company during the mid-1980s.

Over the years Olden saw camera technology improve so that lighting evolved from functionality to art. Cameras in the beginning needed far more light than the naked eye to capture

Figure 3.3 Walter Olden getting the lighting set right.

movement. Progressive decreases in the number of required foot candles—the technical measure of luminescence—meant fewer house lights. With this century's switch to digital technology, the lighting can be as dark as a nightclub, creating a more relaxed and intimate atmosphere with the audience in relative shadow and the performers brightly lit. This more "realistic" lighting, enhanced by the addition of "fog," opens up possibilities for style and artistry that did not exist during the show's earliest days. A greater palette of movement, direction, and colors bring more dramatic emphasis and visual interaction with the musical sound.

Austin City Limits spans decades during which musical performance and visual experiences, whether live or broadcast, were increasingly integrated. At live concerts the performers become a kind of canvas on which the lighting director and technicians ply their art. Television brings different considerations into play. As Olden describes his role, and its relationship to the larger task,

> On TV your peripheral vision is taken down and the director then dictates how you see the show.... Our job is to make it easy for the director to do that, as well as to create some nice dynamics.... We've come to really try to help paint the shot so that the picture is a little more exciting, a little more pleasing as opposed to being bland and basic.[7]

The sound craft, among the greatest achievements of *Austin City Limits*, also links to the visual work. Sound engineer David Hough is the longest running *Austin City Limits* staff member, having helped craft audio for the Willie Nelson pilot.[8] In that period he worked with chief engineer Morgan Martin, who alternated each episode with Hough, one doing the mix and the other acting as the assistant. During this early era, the show's opening sequence included a voice on the talkback microphone over the staged sound check. That voice remains the only way to distinguish Martin from Hough at the helm in those early years. After Season 2, Martin departed and eventually wound up working at George Lucas's Skywalker Ranch. Hough directed the audio thereafter.

Hough recalls his first experience in charge during the Season 1 historic reunion of the Texas Playboys, shortly after the death of their longtime Western swing bandleader Bob Wills. The performance might not have happened if not for the fundraiser held by James White, Alvin Crow, and other local musicians at Austin's famous Broken Spoke to raise money for the Playboys' hotel expenses.[9] Hough suddenly found himself on the hot seat, intimidated both by the number of instruments involved and the sense of gravitas on this historic occasion. "I realized the importance of the fact that these guys reorganized just for this one show," he said. Hough noticed that the lead singer would point at the next musician to take a solo. He realized he could watch for visual cues and turn the fader up before the cameras moved in for the same shot: "That's why I like having the individual camera monitors in here, so I can see what [the cameras] are setting up on."[10]

Hough approaches his task "in layers." He stays more active, with more, in his words, "chasing and nudging" for the television broadcast than happens in a strictly audio recording. "I start off with a basic, kind of a flat-line mix where everything is just settled right in there. And then the things that are interesting that you want to hear are on the next level on top of that." Hough often listens in playback to everything without the lead vocal, or even to the individual instruments, taking joy in "finding the little something

Figure 3.4 David Hough (left) and audio supervisor Sharon Cullen at the console in Studio 6A.

interesting." With complicated setups, for example the one for the jam band Phish, Hough might break the whole apart in order to put the layers back together. His background as a musician also shapes his method: "Being a percussionist, I would just solo up the percussion, listen to the whole song, and if he's doing some little detail...I can reach for that and bring that forward—especially if there's a camera shot on it."

Hough's nearly four decades on *Austin City Limits* encompass several generations of sound-engineering tools. For more than a decade they used an old Studer A-80 16-track and Neve 1073 16-channel deck, equipment that was state-of-the-art for the early 1970s.[11] As Hough remembers, "In those 12 years, the biggest artist we did was Roy Orbison, who had two drummers and a percussion-ist. I had to submix all the drums to one track."[12] Through grants and donations the station invested approximately $2 million in upgraded technology in 1987, including a 24-channel Studer and a 36-channel Neve.[13] Over the years they gained 48 tracks and are now up to 56. Even so the challenges are consistent in some ways to those in the early days. Groups like Pat Metheny and the Dixie Chicks exceed even the current number of channels and require submixing just like Roy Orbison once did. At the other end of the spectrum, a group like the Austin-based Ghostland Observatory produces most of its instrumental sounds from the keyboard, leav-ing Hough in the unusual situation of having one line to a fader. Flashback from this 2007 show to Season 4 (1979), when Esteban Jordan set up a PA onstage, just as he would in a club, with its own small mixer. In that case Hough split Jordan's mono output and made it stereo using "Y cords so we could have some control."

Most dramatic for Hough's work on *Austin City Limits* over the decades, KLRU switched audio technology from analog to digital in 2000 and 2001. Digital sound recording brought new possibilities for manipulating spatial elements: using facets of reverb and room ambiance to add depth, altering the sense of space from front-to-back, left-to-right, and, with modern 5.1 technology, wrapping all the way around. Nonetheless, some older elements of the sound craft stuck around, specifically, in Hough's words, this "really good EMT [Elecktro-Mess-Technik] reverb plate from the '60s that still has tubes in it and that thing's still working today. That's our main sweetener reverb on the lead vocal." Although the 1966 EMT 140 still functions, Hough "discovered that the new theater at the Moody has a very nice reverb itself. Many people have compared its sound to some classic chambers."[14]

Hough enjoys a rare luxury in his television work for *Austin City Limits*: time. He crafts the sound with care and deliberation not common in television audio work, which generally leaves little time for finesse. No other big projects shared the Studio 6A space during its decades at KLRU. That situation remains true even with the new Moody Theater, since tapings feed directly back to the station via fiber optic cable. Hough's results stand out through all the generations of technological change. The show's creator, Bill Arhos, recalled Willie Nelson's reaction to his 1981 PBS special, "Swingin' Over the Rainbow," which honored influential 1930s jazz guitarist Django Reinhardt, as well as earlier Western swing guitar innovators Zeke Campbell and Eldon Shamblin.[15] The show was a follow-up to Nelson's success with early 1980s recordings, *Somewhere Over the Rainbow* and *Always On My Mind*. Upon seeing the finished product, Nelson memorably mused, "Why does it sound better than the album?"[16]

Even Chet Atkins, the Nashville studio and guitar legend, notorious for ruling production at RCA records "with an iron hand," in Arhos's words, trusted *Austin City Limits* with the sound. When his daughter got sick just before his planned return to oversee the editing, Atkins called and said, "You guys know what you're doing, so you go ahead and do it."[17] That said, time alone does not account for the artistry Hough brings to his task. Photographer Scott Newton told me, "I heard that over and over and over and over and over in the dressing rooms and stuff. People talking on the phone, musicians, 'God, you won't believe the sound they get here.' You know, David Hough is directly responsible for that. He's the real hero."[18]

For any given episode, three recordings happen at once: an audio recording, a video recording, and a still photography shoot. In that sense the live audience witnesses multiple performances at once: those by the artists on stage, and those by the people behind the lenses and mikes. Audience members in the studio, for example, can see Scott Newton dance in and around the video camera operators to capture still shots. "Like a gnat," as he puts it, Newton's job is to stay out of the way of the bigger cameras. At the same time the cameras clear a path for his close-up access. In most live performances, a still photographer so near the stage front would be obtrusive. At *Austin City Limits,* however, performers and audience alike accept the presence of the big cameras as part of the gig.

In my conversation with him, Newton searched for an analogy, something along the lines of the small fish that hang out with the whale sharks. He laughed when I suggested "barnacle." "Okay, I'm a barnacle on the ass of the camera man." But then he turned pensive about his role in the whole enterprise: "I'm able to have access to an incredibly intimate still photo shoot of some of the best performers of the twentieth, and now the twenty-first, century and able to immortalize, you know, the spirit that motivates them. I see it as no less than this."

Figure 3.5 Scott Newton has been photographing *Austin City Limits* since Season 5. Many of his works are collected in a book co-edited with Terry Lickona titled *Austin City Limits: 35 Years in Photographs*, put out by University of Texas Press in 2010.

Newton has been photographing *Austin City Limits* since the show's fifth season. Over those decades, he accumulated an impressive portfolio. One of his most famous shots happened during Ray Charles's second appearance on *Austin City Limits* during Season 9 (1984). Typically Newton studies a performer in rehearsal, looking for the "hook shot," the one that will capture the musician's spirit and energy. He had seen Charles rear back at the piano and wail more than once during rehearsal. Newton knew that was the shot he wanted. "And so I framed up for it, got ready for it, and he did it and I was ready for it. And the hair stood up on the back of my neck." Newton's intuition for capturing a performer's best moments matches his technical grasp of form. As he explains, "You see how to tell the story. For example, it's not an accident that the *Austin City Limits* capital set piece is right there at that position. It's not an accident that there's a diagonal running through the shot, there's a 'V' into the viewer. It's not an accident that it's taken from low, [looking] up."[19]

In addition to musicians, Newton also specializes as a freelance political photographer, particularly with Democratic politicians. The same goal drives both musical and political efforts: telling a story with his photographs. Yet the two worlds present opposing

Figure 3.6 Scott Newton's famous image of Ray Charles performing in 1984 on *Austin City Limits*. Photograph by Scott Newton. Courtesy *Austin City Limits*/KLRU-TV.

challenges. The politician should seem accessible and human, whereas the musician should seem heroic or iconic.

Just as in general some people are more photogenic, some performers translate more easily via a still shot than others. A great example of this came on the 2007 summer night when *Austin City Limits* booked a double taping for The Decemberists followed back-to-back by the Austin duo Ghostland Observatory. From behind his still camera lens, Newton takes on a unique perspective. In light of his visual mission, Newton felt like he missed a lot of the aural intricacies of The Decemberists' performance. They struck him as a "subtle listening act.... You get a feeling there's so much lyricism, poetry here that I'm just not getting it because I'm shooting it." Ghostland Observatory, on the other hand, was all charisma and rock-and-roll muscle. They translated through Newton's lens immediately. He says it better: "It didn't matter what the hell they were singing because it was pure spirit up there.... I mean, if you didn't get what he was channeling you are just psychically blind." Newton's photograph, an image of front man Aaron Behrens in motion with his partner Thomas Ross Turner flanked by keyboards in the background, puts across the intensity and energy of their live performance.[20]

The same performance brings almost reverse challenges to people working to capture it via video cameras and microphones. Newton seeks that single two-dimensional picture to encapsulate a powerful performance. The camera crew, on the other hand, captures moving shots over the course of an entire concert. For them pacing and invention are essential. The five-member Decemberists make their job a little easier simply because five band members trading off instruments or taking solos creates more visual variation than two. Likewise Ghostland's instrumental sound feeds mostly through a single instrument, which leaves David Hough

Figure 3.7 Scott Newton photographed The Decemberists during their 2007 performance on *Austin City Limits*. Photograph by Scott Newton. Courtesy *Austin City Limits*/KLRU-TV.

Figure 3.8 That same night, Newton also photographed Ghostland Observatory. Photograph by Scott Newton. Courtesy *Austin City Limits*/ KLRU-TV.

relatively little to do behind the audio board. More instruments and more intricate microphone placement allow him greater control over the final audio quality—more basic ingredients with which to craft his remarkable mix.

Despite the different challenges, a consistent thread binds together everyone working on *Austin City Limits*. Its creative team keeps attuned to capturing the energy, spontaneity, and artistry of musical performance. This goal threads across decades of change in the music, the production style, the technology, and now the studio space itself. When Newton describes his own blend of technique, artistry, and "feel," he sums up what makes the whole show tick:

> You can't see the spirit itself, but you can see the way…the essence modifies the existence that surrounds it, just like a hand in a puppet, just like magnetism on a sheet of paper with iron filings. You can see the pattern. So, okay, you can understand the feel of magnetism. Well, the same thing with spirit. Spirit fleshes out the thing that it gets to inhabit, which is our bodies. So the performer up there, yeah, that's a person in a body, but when they're performing, there's something else. They're channeling that deeper thing. They're channeling the divine. That's what I find interesting, and that's what I'm trying to photograph.[21]

Across decades of change, *Austin City Limits* production staff members continue to pursue "the spirit" or "the muse," and communicate that elusive element of inspired musical performance to those willing to receive it. Director Menotti gets final credit for the production, yet he relies on the artistry of the camera operators, lighting team, audio engineers, editing crew, and others, all

Figure 3.9 Arcade Fire rehearses in Studio 6A on taping day. Doug Robb practices shots on the ped cam to the left, Gary Menotti sits at his small round table with a stopwatch out front, while Scott Newton studies the scene looking for angles of his own.

of whom contribute to the "indefinable chemistry" that ultimately constitutes quality for any television broadcast.[22] Somewhere amid "chemistry" and the "muse," telecommunications becomes art on *Austin City Limits*. Its crew collectively seeks out that sweet spot across the years of changes in music, in its home city, and, ultimately, in the meaning of *Austin City Limits*.

[4]

AUSTIN. IT'S MUSIC TO YOUR EARS

Heading back to the Austin–Bergstrom International Airport on a fairly recent visit, I exited the crawling traffic lanes on Interstate 35 to take an alternate route along Riverside Drive. A homeless man perched on the guard rail alongside the exit caught my eye. He typified Austin's large homeless population: white skin tanned to a dull, leathery texture, frizzed beard brushing against his collarbone, stained army surplus pants rolled to just below the knee. I looked twice at his hand-lettered sign. In black marker scrawled on a piece of brown cardboard, it read, "What's the point in lying? I need a beer."

From a well-educated point of view in my rental car heading to catch an airplane, I was torn. Something akin to admiration for his libertine forthrightness jostled with annoyance at his snarky, low-irony conceit to get beer money by mocking whatever shred of honest compassion might be left for indigent beggars. The backhanded convolution of the little cardboard sign was not only confounding, but typically Austin. In reference to the ubiquitous capital-city bumper sticker and T-shirt slogan that would become subject to copyright conflict, I suppose the man was helping to "Keep Austin Weird."[1] I shook off two fleeting thoughts as I drove past: I wonder if his strategy ever succeeds; and maybe he's hired by the city to stay on the ramps and keep normalcy in the outbound lane of I-35.

As the 1980s dawned, and progressive country no longer resonated as it once had, I imagine *Austin City Limits* poised at a fork in the road: one way led toward the "Austin" in *Austin City Limits* and the other way toward the "country" in progressive country. That last phrase had once connoted so much. It packed complicated and broadly appealing meanings into an economical shorthand and framed the music with the romance of Texas legend and Austin iconoclasm. It communicated a musical space between the overdetermined sounds of country and R&B, along with their love child, rock. Now what? Given the changes in local music, how likely were the same *Austin City Limits* viewers turned on to Alvin Crow during Season 1 ready to embrace The Huns or some other punk band hot in Austin during late 1970s or early 1980s?[2] It seems from this distance not very likely. It must have felt similarly then. Around this time *Austin City Limits* shifted its programming emphasis, at least for a while, more toward country music.

Longtime *Austin City Limits* photographer Scott Newton remembered seasons 5 (1980) and 6 (1981) as "drawing from Nashville." From his perspective, country music filled a void. Looking back on that time years later he reflected that "Texas lost something to say to the rest of the world that was unique, as far as music...I mean, we had [music] here, but we didn't have enough of it to make a TV show out of it, so they imported Nashville. Willie brought his Nashville friends."[3]

The strategy made sense. Nationally country music surged to the pop culture fore during this era, a trend music writer Nick Tosches noted with prescience in the 1977 book *Country: The Biggest Music in America.* The year 1979–1980, the same year *Austin City Limits* taped Season 5, no fewer than 19 movies prominently featured a country song in the soundtrack. These included era blockbusters *Urban Cowboy* and *Every Which Way But Loose*, as well as the small-screen debut of the wildly popular *The Dukes of Hazzard*. The Nashville subgenre "hard country" even subsumed many of progressive country's appealing qualities, like a more basic, stripped-down instrumental sound, an emphasis on classic country instruments like steel guitar and fiddle, and plain-talking lyrics that addressed everyday experiences and emotions.

The void may have seemed more than musical during a time of crisis for station KLRU. A fundraising scandal unrelated to *Austin City Limits* eventually resulted in the station and the University of Texas severing direct ties. In February 1981 the Federal Communications Commission reprimanded the station over fundraising efforts that several years prior had touted a bogus matching donor. That same year the station faced a $500,000 deficit from which it recovered only when a local bank offered a loan. The aftermath resulted in the formation of a nonprofit corporation that still today owns the station, maintains its broadcasting license, and rents studio space from the university.

For its lineup Season 5 highlighted more mainstream Nashville acts than before, including Don Williams and Janie Fricke, Hank Williams Jr., Johnny Paycheck, Mel Tillis, and Billy Joe Shaver, along with country music stalwart Marty Robbins and bluegrass legend Ralph Stanley. Yet at the same time *Austin City Limits* featured performers with local roots. That season aired Texas swing fiddle master Johnny Gimble, as well as episodes devoted to Flaco Jimenez and Beto y Los Fairlanes, Joe Ely and Jerry Jeff Walker, and Gatemouth Brown. An *Austin City Limits* tradition was started when the "Songwriters Special" brought together Willie Nelson, Floyd Tillman, Hank Cochran, Red Lane, Sonny Throckmorton, Whitey Shafer, and Hank Thompson onto one stage. This year also saw Ray Charles and His Orchestra appear for the first time. In many ways, the gumbo variety of the first season remained, if seasoned with more Nashville flavor.

As remarkable as the program itself, press releases about *Austin City Limits* between this and the next major milestone, the show's tenth anniversary, reveal a search for identity. These documents rely on "country music" as a touchstone almost as insistently as the early seasons promoted the notion of Texan-ness. Season 6 promotional materials, for instance, pitch *Austin City Limits* as a country music showcase:

> Tune in for an hour of American country music on *Austin City Limits*...Recorded live in Texas, Austin City Limits features multi-faceted gems of American country music highlighting traditional, bluegrass, contemporary and progressive artists.... Whether you're ready for foot-stompin' honky-tonk or heartwarming ballads, toe-tapping bluegrass or rocking progressive country, you'll hear that and much more on Austin City Limits' great new season.[4]

The actual lineup spanned country acts that ranged from the straight-ahead Nashville pop of Alabama and Lacy J. Dalton (paired with a return of Bobby Bare), to the classic honky-tonk of George Jones and Ray Price, along with next-gen African American honky-tonker Charley Pride; it included the traditional bluegrass of Bill Monroe and "newgrass" of David Grisman as well as the Hollywood-cowboy-revival sounds of Riders in the Sky. It also featured guitar virtuoso Leo Kottke, return appearances by Asleep at the Wheel and Michael Martin Murphey, as well as Joe King Carrasco playing what he called "Texican rock" and Doug Sahm's Sir Douglas Quintet still looking very late 1970s and still playing their sometimes-psychedelic, sometimes-conjunto-influenced rock-and-roll.

During this era Austin journalist John T. Davis interviewed Terry Lickona, who recognized the challenge of the dual identity—a local show with a national audience—facing *Austin City Limits*. Lickona said, "The name of the show was kind of a hang-up at first, because it was perceived as a local program. And now it's sort of a local hang-up because a lot of people around here think it should still be a program that reflects Austin music, and they can't understand why we go outside of Austin to get talent."[5] Austin was not yet so widely acknowledged as a vortex for musical creativity. To revisit Arhos's metaphor once more, the rhino still stood in Austin's bathtub but the out-of-town giraffes looked just as interesting.

The show also wrestled with the hard-to-shake conventional wisdom that media require clear definitions to succeed. Beginning in the 1960s, format radio sealed the notion that if audiences couldn't name it, then they wouldn't buy it, listen to it, or, in the case of television, watch it. Viewers, then, should be less interested in keeping tabs on Austin's live music scene than in seeing a program that fit their preconceived expectations. Lickona said as much at the time to Davis at the city's newspaper: "Our national audience continues to grow, but they also continue to expect some kind of country music. They don't care if new wave or jazz or R&B is what is happening in Austin right now. They're used to tuning in and seeing some kind of country act."[6] Lickona remains the heart and soul of *Austin City Limits* decades later, partly for the way he gracefully navigates tugs from every direction, and partly for the way his outlook evolved with the show over the years.

Seasons 7 and 8 continued to lean heavily on Nashville-based acts, but slipped in a few striking musical outliers as well. The twelfth episode of Season 7, for example, paired Pete Fountain with a group called the Jazzmanian Devils as well as George Thorogood and Dave Olney, neither of whom fit even an expansive definition of country music. Season 8 included hour-long performances by B.B. King and Roy Orbison. B.B. King's episode, in particular, stands out as one of the all-time greats.[7] Yet in the early 1980s the booking bucked against the language in press releases that tried to corral the show into a country music framework. Season 9 (1984) in particular represented a peak in the tension between performer line-ups and the promotional language that described them. A sample page from the press kit sets out clear genre terms:

> It's an hour of country music at its best!...From deep in the heart of Texas comes Austin City Limits' exciting new season! It's the best in country music featuring top artists singing traditional, contemporary, and progressive styles.... From traditional to progressive country, from blues to bluegrass, travel the music spectrum when Austin City Limits returns for an exciting ninth season! New and old, established and upcoming ...stay tuned for an hour of the best of country music on Austin City Limits.[8]

Yet this same season opened with a return visit by Ray Charles and closed with another long-since-cherished performance by Stevie Ray Vaughan, draped in a blue-and-white kimono-style shirt, hat brim pulled low over his eyes, playing blues as though he was an otherworldly musical conduit.[9] Scattered in between were some "top artists singing traditional, contemporary, and progressive styles" from both Nashville and the local Texas scene, including Gail Davies, Lee Greenwood, George Strait, and Johnny Rodriguez. A "country music legends" special brought together

Faron Young, Kitty Wells, Johnny Wright, the Sons of the Pioneers, Joe and Rose Maphis, Pee Wee King and Red Stewart, and the Collins Sisters. Other Season 9 artists like Jerry Lee Lewis, Bonnie Raitt, and Sleepy LeBeef, as well as Jimmy Buffett, all stood outside the country music mold.

It is curious why press releases emphasized country music so insistently even as the programming ventured further afield. It is yet more puzzling when the term abruptly disappears from promos beginning in Season 10 (1985). Through all its phases, great bookings happened as they happened on *Austin City Limits* regardless of whether or not the acts fit neat musical categories. But the language for promoting *Austin City Limits* changed in significant ways during this era. Country music moved aside as a conceptual framework to make room for a newly acknowledged historical weight, noteworthy for the program and for its home city as well. Instead of country music, the Season 10 press copy emphasizes longevity and a self-conscious sense of history: "It's public television's longest-running music program.... For ten years, the place to go for the best in traditional and contemporary music has been Austin City Limits.... For ten years Austin City Limits has captured the best that contemporary and traditional music has to offer."[10]

A decade was something to celebrate indeed. As Arhos looked back years later, he recalled the sense of achievement. *Austin City Limits*, by that time the oldest live music program on television, enjoyed an established national presence, ranking among the top 10 in every audience category for PBS and number one for a couple of demographic groups. To mark the anniversary, a special outdoor event headlined by the Texas Playboys was staged on Austin's Congress Avenue.

While the press copy espoused a new emphasis on history, the season that followed still favored mainstream country acts: Oak

Ridge Boys, Waylon Jennings, Billy Joe Shaver, Eddie Rabbitt, Tammy Wynette, The Judds, Glen Campbell, Juice Newton, Larry Gatlin, Earl Thomas Conley, and Vince Gill. Outside the country music center, singer-songwriters Mark Gray and Nanci Griffith, and bluegrass singer and mandolin master Ricky Skaggs performed. Neil Young, with an hour-long performance on Season 10's second episode, stood apart from these artists, as did native Texans Joe Ely and Eric Johnson. Yet aside from the show's name and the chorus of "London Homesick Blues," overt references to both country music and Texas identity evaporated.

The shift of language came in part from changing tastes. A musical style can seem so hip one year only to turn stale the next. By the mid-1980s country music remained a strong Nashville-centered industry but had lost its status as the nation's pop culture flavor of the day. As quickly as country flooded the popular music landscape, it subsided again—so it goes with musical fashion. Other forces of change ran deeper.

Radical technology developments roughly coincide with the shift in *Austin City Limits* promos and explain broader dynamics in US popular music at the time. The birth of compact disc (CD) digitization sparked the re-release of vast stores of older music. Historic recordings of blues and country, Cajun, conjunto, and other styles all simultaneously connected oral folk traditions (like the ones that once interested John Lomax) with new audiences and, thus, new potential for profit. A growing number of musicians carried on a similar spirit, straddling artistic success and commercial appeal at once. Likewise more and more of their releases overlapped established record-bin (or CD-bin) boundaries dividing one genre from another.

Programming-wise, things held steady for a while. Season 12 (1987), for example, included mainstream country stars like

Ronnie Milsap and Randy Travis, but also classic, more liminal performers like Brenda Lee and Johnny Cash with June Carter, Tommy Cash & The Carter Family. Texas-based musicians Lyle Lovett and The Fabulous Thunderbirds appeared that year, as did Leon Russell and Steve Earle who paired for the fourth episode, followed by a full hour of Fats Domino. The ninth episode, dubbed the "Squeezebox Special," featured accordionists Queen Ida, Santiago Jimenez Jr., and Ponty Bone, all practicing different traditions on the instrument. Season 13 (1988) presented a similar mix: with Reba McEntire, Larry Gatlin, and Holly Dunn aiming pretty much down the middle, while Loudon Wainwright III and Leo Kottke fleshed things out in a way less easy to pin down. Stanley Jordan gave an hour-long performance in Season 14 (1989), as did Leonard Cohen in his first and famous US television appearance.

While the lineups maintained continuity with recent seasons, the years between the tenth and fifteenth anniversaries were transitional for the city of Austin in ways that bear on *Austin City Limits*. Civic groups began to form around the growing realization that music's central place in local life might suggest a potentially more critical place for it within the local economy. The Austin Music Industry Council (AMIC) formed in 1986 with the stated intent "to forge an alliance between Austin's music industry and its business community ... and provide resources for the development and growth of music industry infrastructure necessary for Austin's expansion as a major music center."[11] The founding document cites a study from the previous year, commissioned by the Austin Chamber of Commerce and conducted by SRI International, that identified music as a special aspect of the city's arts culture. The AMIC sponsored workshops about taxes, accounting, and other music business issues, as well as tours of local studios, including one in November 1987 sponsored by "AMIC and Arlyn Studios, courtesy of Freddie [sic] Joe Fletcher." Fletcher, nephew to Willie Nelson, would play a key role in the development of the ACL Live Music Venue and the W Hotel complex two decades later.

By 1987 members could join AMIC for $20.00, a fee that included a T-shirt and a bumper sticker that read "Austin Music— You Make It Live," or, later, "Austin. It's music to your ears."[12] AMIC connected with music business activities like SXSW, first held in 1987, and other local groups like the Sixth Street Conservation Society. They kept tabs on local music events like Aqua Fest, which that year featured mostly Austin bands and attracted 250,000 people. That same year the Austin-based regional public television service bifurcated into two distinct stations, with KLRU focusing on the Austin community and KLRN serving San Antonio, reclaiming the original call letters to do so. KLRU's growing sense of wherewithal mirrors that which characterized the city of Austin more and more as the 1980s progressed.[13] In 1989 AMIC Secretary Mike Workman reported the impact of the music industry to be worth $75 million to the city economy.[14] By mid-1990s reports, the number would climb to $400 million for the annual Austin economy.[15] A more recent study lumped music as part of the "creative sector" that also included film, gaming, and visual arts, and brought "$4.35 billion in economic activity in 2010."[16]

In addition to AMIC, other groups from different corners of the city also fostered music's vital place in civic life and civic identity. These organizations included the Austin chapter of the Texas Music Association, Austin Lawyers and Accountants for the Arts, the local Federation of Musicians, the Music Umbrella of Austin, and others. So many pockets of leadership within the city contributed toward, even as they contested, a shared vision for music: all working to make sure the rhinoceros in the bathtub stayed put and that more and more people knew about it. In fact Austin's pervasive civic engagement may be the element distinguishing it from places like Athens, Georgia, and Seattle, Washington, which saw noteworthy music scenes bloom and fade as progressive country once did in Austin. Though remarkable music still happens in those communities, the special moment came and went. Likewise Austin never recaptured its progressive country moment nor, for that matter, its punk rock moment in the 1980s. Nevertheless it gradually established a sustained reputation as a lively place for music. *Austin City Limits* spread that impression farther than it might otherwise have reached.

By the time Austin officially adopted "Live Music Capital of the World," on August 29, 1991,[17] it was a veritable statement of purpose. The slogan shaped city-level decisions at crucial junctures for decades to come. For example, when it came time to build a new airport (which opened in May 1999), the Request for Proposals (RFP) stated the city's desire to feature not only Austin restaurants and retailers but also musicians. In the Austin–Bergstrom International Airport, music today makes the first and last impression on travelers. The airport features daily live "Music in the Air" in the concourse and in restaurants such as Western swing frontman par excellence Ray Benson's Roadhouse and legendary Houston Oiler running back Earl Campbell's Sports Bar. Retail establishments include a store named for two music-related Austin icons, Waterloo Records and, of course, *Austin City Limits*. More recently the city played a major role in building the new *Austin City Limits* music venue. The RFP specified that development proposals for Block 21, the last pristine piece of city-owned downtown real estate, should include at least one nonprofit enterprise. *Austin City Limits* ultimately fit the bill.[18]

By its fifteenth anniversary, *Austin City Limits* was its home city's most famous cultural representative.[19] It was the primary way that people in Hoboken or Juneau or San Diego knew Austin as a music-loving town. By then *Austin City Limits* stood among the longest-running programs of any kind on television, either public or commercial. Longtime camera operator Robert Moorhead told me, "For years *Gunsmoke* was our big competition because it was the longest-running series on television. I think we've beat them out now."[20] Station KLRU rested on solid financial ground, and boasted dramatic increases in local viewership and monetary donations.

They staged another celebration to mark the milestone anniversary, with Chet Atkins originally scheduled to headline. Dr. Red

Figure 4.1 Longtime camera operator Robert Moorhead stands before the *Austin City Limits* signing wall on the second floor of station KLRU, a memorial to a long-cherished tradition for staff members and artists.

Duke, the trauma surgeon turned public figure via the nationally syndicated "Texas Health Reports," played host. Tied up at
a recording engagement in London, Atkins cancelled at the last
minute. Leo Kottke filled in, and Arhos reported that "about 5,000
people came and it did a lot to help the station."[21] According to
the bemused description printed in the *Dallas Morning News*, the
event took on a peculiarly local tone, genuflecting toward the origins of *Austin City Limits* for a hometown audience: "Onstage,
Gary P. Nunn and the Lost Gonzo Band—resplendent in cowboy
hats, boots and armadillo bolo ties—are belting out Lennon–
McCartney's *Birthday* to a slightly befuddled audience at the
Palmer Auditorium. Lyle Lovett and Marsha [sic] Ball are singing
background vocals. So too, for that matter, is Dr. Red Duke of the
University of Texas Health Science Center."[22]

The program itself, meanwhile, embarked on a "roots music"
phase around this time, though the phrase itself only gradually
worked into the vocabulary of people speaking for the show. Roots
suggested an inclusive, in-between approach to *Austin City Limits*
programming, one that arguably always characterized the program's contents but now seemed easier to talk about in those terms.
Around the fifteenth anniversary, Terry Lickona told a *Houston
Post* writer, "We have a strong prejudice toward singer-songwriter
types.... You can't say they're country, rock, pop or folk. It's not as
simple as that anymore."[23] That same year he talked to an Austin
reporter about bringing balance to each season's bookings: "We
work hard to make sure there are different types of music, from
bluegrass, contemporary and traditional country to blues and folk,
and that there's also a sexual and ethnic balance. It gets pretty
complicated sometimes, but we keep at it until we're satisfied the
final product meets our criteria."[24] The next year he mused over
the dynamics between the show and broader music industry

categories when he pointed out to a reporter, "*Billboard* magazine called it a 'pop music series,' although that article was in their country section."[25]

Arhos remembered that Terry Lickona always wanted to make *Austin City Limits* "more eclectic," and the cards fell into place to make that possible around the early 1990s: "And then, you know, once the country music scene kind of took a secondary position, and it wasn't as hot as it was in the 70s and early 80s, there was no reason not to branch it out."[26] By then "roots music" and "Americana" entered common parlance to describe a musical mixed bag, a cross section of performers (black, white, and brown) and sounds (country, blues, R&B, and rock-and-roll). These words crop up in *Austin City Limits* press releases and slogans during the 1990s, and, for a time, fit both its contemporary reality and its sense of history all the way back to the beginning.

Roots music, as a label, stretched wide enough to cover generations of Texas regional sounds by the likes of Marcia Ball and Gary P. Nunn or Lyle Lovett, but could also account for the jazz-oriented banjo playing of someone like Bela Fleck, who appeared in Season 17 (1992).[27] "Roots" linked artists with sounds as different as C.J. Chenier, Son Volt, and B.B. King, Ruthie Foster and Loretta Lynn, Santiago Jimenez and Tish Hinojosa, and arranged them along a continuous conceptual thread. Under the "roots" umbrella *Austin City Limits* valued country music as one among an array of core American musical styles. "Roots" demarcated an intellectual space where Larry Gatlin or Chet Atkins could dwell comfortably with Tom Waits and Fats Domino.

For a time Lickona used the term to explain his expansive vision for *Austin City Limits* during conversations with reporters. In 1993, for example, Lickona described the programming as "a mix or balance of original music that reflects a variety of styles that are uniquely American. It's sort of slanted toward roots music, for want of a better label, and captures the flavor of Texas music and the Austin style of presenting and appreciating music."[28] Three years later, in 1996, he summed it up as "a showcase for American music of all types, with an emphasis on what I call roots music—country, conjunto, blues, Cajun and other styles you can't really classify."[29]

Despite its widespread prevalence and its resonance with *Austin City Limits* programming, "roots" ultimately lacked staying power as musical terminology. By the decade's end the term lost its connotative zing, dissipating gradually into subcategories tangled up with the older musical conceptions it once challenged: roots country, roots rock, roots of the blues, and so on. Lickona reflected years later on the term's lost semantic potency:

> Today, especially if you were to ask somebody younger what they consider roots music to mean, they would think of old-time music, traditional music as in traditional blues or traditional folk or acoustic-type music, bluegrass, etc. I think that's how a lot of people today would perceive roots music to be. And that wasn't our intention at all. We never limited what the definition of roots music was to that extent.[30]

For the show's promotion staff during the 1990s, "roots music" and "Americana" gave way to ever-broadening language. They tried using no slogan at all in 1995. By 1998 slogans included "All-American Music" and "Where Music Lives." Yet roots left behind a significant conceptual legacy for both the show and its city. Roots for a while suggested a fresh way of thinking about *Austin City Limits* music, just as it did within the music industry more broadly. It evoked the worthwhile romance of returning to how things began rather than dwelling on how they have developed. It suggested a cache of category-defying "genuine" experiences and untrammeled "authentic" naturalness, ready for discovery by those seeking to tap the deepest currents of innovation. When it came to musicians, roots pointed to the quality— irrespective of commercial success—of integrating antecedent repertoire, style, or method with something fresh, a quality that distinguished an artist from the late-twentieth-century musical hoi polloi.

Despite the fact that roots as a term faded out, the in-between space it demarcated lingered for Austin, which took on the character of a city that could straddle both artistic and commercial values. Austin's two best-known cultural entities attest to this dynamic. In addition to *Austin City Limits*, people know Austin for its music industry conference South by Southwest (SXSW) which began in 1987. Taken together, *Austin City Limits* and SXSW stake out opposite poles that secure Austin's eminence as, at once, a place for true music lovers whose passions resist the flighty winds of the popular music business, and a mecca for musicians who crave popular music success. One SXSW chronicler for *Billboard* magazine captured the tension well in his opening to a 1998 piece, first describing an outdoor cookout at the home of Texas musician Joe Ely, who had recently released *Twistin' in the Wind*. He writes:

> The relaxed tableau provided stark contrast to the industry bustle that was overwhelming downtown Austin, where the streets on this Friday afternoon of the South By Southwest music conference were swarming with movers and shakers, expense accounters, cellular phoners, indie hustlers—the kind

of frenzied folks whose aggressive attitudes stamped them as conventioneers rather than natives.[31]

In short, the hard-edged music industry types infiltrated Austin for a couple of weeks at SXSW, long enough to get the necessary jobs accomplished, but not long enough to kill the unperturbed, authentic spirit of the place.

Sociologist and cultural theorist Pierre Bourdieu once said, "We know that to name is to show, to create, to bring into existence."[32] Bourdieu also introduced the notion of "cultural capital," sometimes symbolic capital, as a way to conceive the significance and sometimes contradictory meanings of people or works of art, cities or media institutions.[33] In some sense *Austin City Limits* and the city of Austin elevated the cultural capital of one another. Each nudged the other into existence. Music-loving, relaxed, nonmaterialistic, hip, independent, real: these are among the characteristics of the Austin "natives" conjured above and begin to pinpoint the kind of cultural capital Austin still enjoys. At the start of *Austin City Limits,* Austin enjoyed fame for music clubs like the Armadillo World Headquarters that rested at a hip junction between commercialism and artistry. *Austin City Limits* projected that sensibility on television to a wide audience. Though the progressive country scene changed, Austin continued to skate a similar duality with regard to its civic identity, just as it continued to intersect and overlap the range of symbolic meanings contained within *Austin City Limits.*

If the balance between commerce and art remains relevant for *Austin City Limits,* and it does, then it flows from two directions in the current era. A major music festival bearing the program's name and a high-tech studio/venue space housed in a fancy hotel in a tony new entertainment district bolster the first element. Years of consistent and quality production, underscored by the broader media framework of PBS, sustain the second. The twenty-fifth anniversary stands as a turning point for *Austin City Limits,* when it took on the quality of an idea, or a brand, with deep roots and the potential to bloom in multiple directions at once.

[5]

A PLACE TO DISCOVER MUSIC

Once upon a time getting to see a live taping of *Austin City Limits* was no easy matter. If you lacked good connections, then you waited by the radio for the announcer to say where and when to find the space-available tickets. With tickets in hand, you arrived early, snagged a parking spot (a rarity on the University of Texas campus), and secured a place in the line winding its way across the large concrete courtyard at the Jesse H. Jones Communications Center plaza. As the hour approached you held your breath as the two small elevators clambered their way to the sixth floor and back, hoping your turn came before Studio 6A reached the fire marshal's limit. All remaining ticket holders would go home disappointed.

Triumphant, you emerged from the elevator, greeted by the wall of framed photos—Bonnie Raitt and B.B. King and Flaco Jimenez and Dave Matthews and Dolly Parton—all performing against the familiar faux Austin skyline. You followed these to the beer table where a volunteer handed you a plastic cup of Ziegenbock, Budweiser's regional brew-brand answer to Texas's Shiner beer. You entered the chilly, darkened studio and found a seat, anticipating the moment when Terry Lickona would mount the stage, thank the sponsors, and begin the show. While you waited you studied the wooden backdrop, an approximate rendering of Austin's early

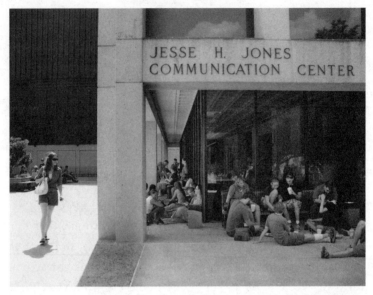

Figure 5.1 *Austin City Limits* ticket holders wait patiently in the long line that snakes around the Communications complex, rechristened for Jesse H. Jones in 1982.

1980s skyline with construction cranes painted in later to signify the city's rapid expansion. This space looks so much smaller in person than it does on TV. Only the chalk-drawn lines on the well-worn floors keep the standing audience out of the camera operators' way.

After 36 seasons, all that changed. On February 24, 2011, *Austin City Limits* opened a new studio home at the Moody Theater. It was part of the W Hotel Complex on Second, across from City Hall, a stretch now renamed "Willie Nelson Boulevard." The Moody Theater holds nearly tenfold the capacity of Studio 6A, yet no seat is more than 75 feet from the stage and the sight lines are impeccable.[1] All three floors include multiple bars, a total of twelve in all.

On the second level Scott Newton's photographs of *Austin City Limits* performers, beginning with Season 5, line the walls.

Figure 5.2 The crowd waits before a double taping for K'Naan and Mos Def in Studio 6A. Terry Lickona is standing on the bleacher steps to the right in the photo.

The modest 8 by 10 frames are gone. Here Newton's photos cover the walls as they would in a gallery, clustered in different sizes and formats—some black and white, some color, some on canvas, others smooth and glossy and smartly framed. This is a dream showcase for a photographer's corpus. Upstairs another gallery space for rotating exhibits occupies the third-floor lobby walls. The first show featured photos from the estate of the late iconic rock photographer Jim Marshall. Co-sponsored by Jack Daniels, this inaugural two-year run began in fall 2011. It would have been hard to imagine the elaborate new digs and steep upgrades in 1974. However, the decades passed and the show's popularity grew. Changes took shape on the horizon as the twentieth century drew to a close.

Substantive modifications began in the early 1990s, when *Austin City Limits* planners updated the show. They replaced Nunn's version of "London Homesick Blues" with one by John Mills that sounded more polished. They updated the famous skyline backdrop, originally painted from a 1980 photograph of downtown Austin. First appearing on the August 3, 1981 show, it included two landmark silhouettes, the Texas State Capitol and the University of Texas tower, spaced more closely together than in real life. Because of this backdrop, television viewers often assumed the tapings took place outdoors.

Critical appreciation for *Austin City Limits* picked up momentum during the 1990s. Even before the decade started, *New York Times* music critic Jon Pareles, writing in 1989, reflected on a broadcast of singer-songwriter John Hiatt paired with Los Lobos, the Mexican American band out of Los Angeles. The program's straightforward production style struck Pareles most. He wrote, "'Austin City Limits' has quietly outlived other pop-concert television shows by keeping things simple. The program books performers on grounds other than raw popularity, seeking out the deserving individualists who tend to land in the middle and lower reaches of the pop charts. And the show...simply puts those performers on a stage and lets them play, uninterrupted and unglossed."[2]

As the decade progressed, the musical breadth of *Austin City Limits* continued garnering critical attention from multiple corners. Station KLRU and *Austin City Limits* received the "Keeping the Blues Alive" media award from the Blues Foundation in 1998, the nonperformer equivalent of the W. C. Handy awards. The occasion sparked Terry Lickona's reflection on the history of the blues on *Austin City Limits* in a press release for a TV special on August 12 of that year:

Figure 5.3 In a photo taken during Mos Def's rehearsal, the paint and light bulbs screwed into the faux-Austin backdrop in Studio 6A look much different than they did on TV.

Originally *Austin City Limits* aimed to showcase Texas-based singers and pickers like Delbert McClinton and Lightnin' Hopkins, but the real break-through came when B.B. King took the stage in 1982.... At the time B.B. had recorded a country-flavored album in Nashville, so we reasoned he would come and give us his take on country.... Instead, it was classic B.B., a down-and-dirty blues show—not to mention it was one of the best *ACL* shows we had ever seen.[3]

Writing for the *Chicago Tribune* in 1998, television critic Steve Johnson characterized its contents as "Americana and Texas folk-alternative country" and "a granddaddy to the loose but growing genre known as Americana." But then he said more:

The show, a public TV stalwart with nearly a two-and-a-half decade history, is that exception in the niche-happy world of modern popular music, a genre-bender. It has a knack for finding artists from the cutting edge of country, folk and blues. And it gives them, as well as neglected legends and just enough mainstreamers to maintain the balance, a pristine, half-hour showcase.[4]

That same year, Season 23, *Austin City Limits* aired an eclectic range of artists including bluesman Buddy Guy, country icon Loretta Lynn, the Indigo Girls, the vocal jazz group Manhattan Transfer, as well as a tribute to Townes van Zandt and an episode bringing together Marcia Ball, Irma Thomas, and Tracy Nelson.

In light of *Austin City Limits* history and, particularly, the fate of *Soundstage*, its closest competitor during the previous decade, being celebrated as a "genre-bender" was noteworthy. *Soundstage* began in Chicago at around the same time as *Austin City Limits* and, like its Austin contender, crafted a high-quality program that aired a free mix of musical performances. Its first production run halted in 1985. (It was resurrected in 2003 but ended its second run in 2010.) At the time *Soundstage* ran aground, its fate suggested the dangers of trying to sustain an audience in the absence of clear genre boundaries.

Musical media long assumed that listeners or, in this case, viewers, judge music by common style and sound features that allow it to fall neatly into a genre.[5] During the 1980s, its hazy categories seemed explanation enough for the demise of *Soundstage*. Lickona then told *Austin Chronicle* writer Marybeth Gradziel that the fallen competitor "presented so many different styles of music that it didn't hold the same audience from week to week. That's something we have taken note of, but we're not shaping *Austin City Limits* based on the lack of *Soundstage* success."[6]

In that same interview Lickona expressed frustration over the constraints of genre. He said, "frankly, if I had my way, a fantasy in this real world, I'd love to feature all kinds of music in every style and every corner of America and beyond, but we do have to stay within a certain format. We have to be consistent."[7] Within a decade that eclectic vision appeared more within reach. Into the twenty-first century, *Austin City Limits* staked out an ever-broadening musical niche. Getting there meant navigating turbulent waters—pressures from without and upheavals from within—during the late 1990s, leading to the show's twenty-fifth anniversary.

Encroaching competition from cable and, increasingly, the Internet, provoked a broadcast television crisis during the 1990s. The intrusion forced all three major commercial networks, along with PBS, to alter strategies in order to stay viable. PBS restructured its program distribution in a way that shook the foundations of *Austin City Limits*. In short, PBS removed the show from its package of standard subscription offerings to public station members. Instead they offered *Austin City Limits* as part of the newly launched PBS Select package, a concept similar to the different tiers for premium versus regular channels offered by cable companies.[8] PBS Select occupied the third and most expensive tier, below the basic package of PBS shows called the National Program Service, and also below the second PBS Plus level.[9]

Stations wanting to air *Austin City Limits* now paid extra, based on a sliding scale. In this new system a station in a Memphis-sized market would have to pay $4,000 for a season, while a larger market like Miami shelled out an extra $10,000; WNET in New York owed an additional $30,000 to $35,000 for the program.[10] As a result, *Austin City Limits* began to lose subscribers where struggling local public stations could not afford the added expense. The number of stations carrying the program dropped nearly 30 percent—from 255 to 175—between seasons 22 and 23 (1997–1998).[11]

Austin City Limits temporarily survived the loss in station subscriptions due to underwriters such as Ford, Budweiser, and the Tourism Division of the Texas Department of Commerce. These sponsors took up the slack for a while, but decreased exposure threatened those financial relationships in the long term. In other words, the drop in programming distribution made it harder to convince sponsors that *Austin City Limits* played to a nationwide audience. Clearly something had to give to resolve the financial disconnect between attracting national sponsorship and losing station subscriptions.

Amid these external pressures, internal changes also occurred at KLRU. In 1998 the Board of Directors hired Mary Beth Rogers as CEO when Bill Arhos retired as General Manager of the station. She brought different strengths to the job. Across more than two decades, Arhos had forged deep connections in the music and broadcasting worlds, particularly within the Country Music Association and the institutional hierarchy of PBS. In the latter organization his role extended beyond advocating for *Austin City Limits*. As a longtime member of its Board of Directors he helped shape PBS programming more generally.

Rogers had little previous music or broadcasting expertise, but brought a mind for strategy shaped by her political work, particularly as chief of staff for Texas Governor Ann Richards. She approached the task as "a public service agency just like government work," and restructured operations at the station.[12] She also engaged the city of Austin in new ways. Arhos credited Rogers with connecting the dots between the city's efforts to boost the music economy and *Austin City Limits*. Referring to members of Austin's Chamber of Commerce, he told me, "I think Mary Beth finally convinced them.... They didn't have a clue. They had no idea what kind of impact the program had economically on this city."[13]

Austin City Limits managers began thinking in "brand" new ways. In 1998 board chair Robin Shivers wrote a memo to decision-makers at Busch, Anheuser Busch, and Brown Distributing, promoting sponsorship renewal for Season 24 (1999).[14] In it she asserted that "PBS is considered the second most powerful media brand behind Disney." Another internal change corroborated this shifting mindset when Ed Bailey entered the *Austin City Limits* scene, at first to oversee events anticipated for the approaching twenty-fifth anniversary. A marketing specialist with a love of music, Bailey left Cleveland's Rock and Roll Hall of Fame to take the KLRU job. He brought to Austin's public television station the Darwinian perspective of a businessperson: *Austin City Limits* (and PBS, for that matter) would either adapt to the new conditions of the television industry or cease to function. In 1999, the following year, he stepped into the newly created position of Vice President for Brand Development at KLRU.

The conceptual shift from *Austin City Limits* as a television show to *Austin City Limits* as a "media brand" occurred around the milestone Season 25. Ed Bailey's new job entailed nurturing the concept of *Austin City Limits,* sometimes now *ACL,* as a brand, and ensuring its broad and effective circulation within the contemporary media-rich cultural environment. His hiring signals the way *Austin City Limits* leadership not only newly acknowledged the show's sense of legacy, but also began assuming more deliberate control over its long-term relevance and viability.

That said, *Austin City Limits* was no stranger to entrepreneurial strategy. Writer Clifford Endres reported on a plan in 1989, ultimately unrealized, for Republic of Texas Communications to "repackage highlights from the first 10 years and offer them to more than 2,500 outlets, potentially expanding the *Austin City Limits* audience by tens of millions."[15] The next year *Austin City Limits* experimented with an offshoot half-hour program called *The Texas Connection*, featuring Texas-based bands, funded by and aired on cable's *Nashville Network*. Co-produced by Lickona and Arhos, the show lasted four seasons. Even before then *Austin City Limits* belt buckles or lapel pins had circulated every now and then.[16] T-shirts and hats still do.

Arhos had always sought creative ways to leverage ancillary rights from *Austin City Limits* toward new income for the station.[17] In the later 1990s, KLRU partnered with Legacy/Columbia Records to produce several compilations from the *Austin City Limits* archives. These included *The Best of Austin City Limits: Country Music's Finest Hour* in 1996, *Legends of Country Music: The Best of Austin City Limits* in 1997, and the *ACL Big Blues Extravaganza: The Best of Austin City Limits* in 1998. According to its press release, the latter DVD "corrals 15 Blues tracks from longest-Running Pop Music Series" and spans approximately 20 years, beginning with Lightnin' Hopkins in 1978 and ending with Keb' Mo' in 1996. It encompasses "bluesmen and blues women who were either born in Texas, passed through, made it their home or took a taste of the Lone Star State back on the road with them."[18] Two tunes in particular represent *Austin City Limits'* typical range: B.B. King's performance of the Willie Nelson song "Night Life" in 1982 and Stevie Ray Vaughan's "Lovestruck Baby," which first appeared on his 1983 debut album, *Texas Flood*.

These efforts generated some profits for the station. Yet they were only a meager foretaste of the radical re-evaluation of *Austin City Limits* around its twenty-fifth anniversary. Changes in leadership, the creation of the new VP position, and the adoption of the concept of "brand" all signaled a move to keep *Austin City Limits* vital, to keep it from becoming relegated to a DVD retrospective.

KLRU then made a gutsy move. Rationalization for it survives in a contemporary report, an undated document titled "Executive Summary of Programmers Survey."[19] The document established that 74 percent of the total possible PBS stations aired the program in Season 24, then questioned whether or not stations would still carry the program were it free of charge. Its findings proposed a drastically transformed approach, which Ed Bailey explained years later:

> We told PBS "we want out." We went to a national PBS conference in San Francisco, and…we announced that *Austin City Limits* on its 25th anniversary is coming back to all stations, and it's coming back to you free of charge. We gave it away to get back on the air. We got out of the syndication business.… Instead of saying, "Hey, we're bringing in Garth Brooks and the Dixie Chicks, you should pay us for this," we went completely opposite of this and said, "We've got to give it away, we've got to get shelf space." That's market lingo…you can't have a transaction if you're not on the shelf.[20]

Austin City Limits thus broke from the PBS system. It offered the show free to every station, choosing to rely solely on sponsorship for funding. In terms of potential subscription revenue lost, it was a $360,000 gamble to get back "on the shelf." The risk turned out to be a good one.

For *Austin City Limits* to step outside normal PBS protocol and seek economic independence required a conceptual leap. It came as something like an epiphany about the show's singularity, following decades of programming and decades of finding words to describe and promote it. Perhaps that sense of historical self-real-ization that budded around the tenth anniversary simply reached full bloom 15 years later. This meant reckoning *Austin City Limits* as more than a television series. It had become an institution for music, for television media, and for its home city.

Preconceptions about the show's contents lingered in some corners of the PBS world. It proved troublesome in the 1990s, for example, when some audiences, particularly PBS powers-that-be, found the show's country music associations hard to slough. Bailey recalled that Detroit public television station WTVS refused to air it "because they thought we were too country," even after *Austin City Limits* became free.[21] Bill Arhos attributed the situation to the complacency of PBS station programmers who penciled in pro-grams and checked the ratings, but failed to take time to view the actual content: "I'd be standing in the back at meetings for pro-grammers where they would take tapes to show and Ray Charles would come on. People would say 'I didn't know they had people like Ray Charles on *Austin City Limits*.'" He went on to chuckle that "the PBS people…some of them probably still think it's coun-try. Alabama probably just now found out."[22]

Perhaps it was "a legacy tied to the term 'Austin, Texas.'"[23] Maybe country music itself had gathered too much moss and *Austin City Limits* suffered by association. The "anything but coun-try" phenomenon of contemporary metropolitan taste was an hon-est reaction to the veneer of insincerity Nashville country courted at the end of the 1980s.[24] Whatever the reason, the lingering coun-try music tinge mattered little in practical terms until PBS, amid syndication upheaval, introduced a slick new competitor in 1997 called *Sessions at West 54th*.

Doomsayers predicted difficulties for *Austin City Limits*. More often than not these dire forecasts from different camps were based on country music's waning popularity despite the fact that the country music emphasis had disappeared from press releases over a decade before. *Austin City Limits* had actively and deliberately expanded its audience base for years. As Lickona told a reporter in mid-decade, "Our job is to advocate musical palates.... Diverse bookings help us reach a wider audience. The best example of that is the (1989) Leonard Cohen show."[25] Whereas Vince Gill and Tammy Wynette appeared in Season 20 (1995), so too did the Neville Brothers and Iris DeMent. Where there was Alison Krauss and a classic episode with Roger Miller and Marty Robbins in Season 21 (1996), there was also Los Lobos or Keb' Mo' or a classic episode of Roy Orbison. And so on.

An Austin newspaper article titled "Upstaged?" quoted Alan Foster, the vice president of fundraising and syndicated programs for PBS: "'Austin City Limits' hasn't been 100 percent country music for some time, but in the minds of programmers it remains our country music show. Some shows just aren't programs that are 'national.' But 'Austin City Limits' is a very important show to the markets that want it."[26] The slogan for the show in 1997 might be taken as a direct response to Foster: "Not just country music, *your country's* music."[27]

Sessions at West 54th used a concert format similar to that of *Austin City Limits* but added a notable personality acting as host. It used glossy, faster-moving production values and enjoyed financial bankrolling by Sony Music, whose Manhattan address gave the program its name. High quality though it was, the contender lasted only three seasons. If *Soundstage* once fell victim to genre ambiguity, *Sessions* failed because it came across as too baldly commercial for its PBS forum. Arhos flatly told me, "You understand that [show] was commercial."[28] Thus *Sessions* was like a flashy fish out of water in the PBS media pond. A critical balance between commercial savvy and artistic authenticity, so key to *Austin City Limits*, was off for *Sessions*.

Austin City Limits works as an idea and a symbol, both in and outside the boundaries of the weekly hour-long televised episode. Not surprisingly Ed Bailey best articulates *Austin City Limits* as it exists beyond the television series: a concept, a multifaceted idea with meaning in constant flux but whose core consists of a quality musical experience that cuts across, if not defies, genre. *ACL* in this most recent era has moved from a PBS television show that features good music to "a place to discover music…a place that connects artists and fans," including, but not limited to, the program.[29]

Genre still operates on *Austin City Limits* as it does elsewhere. We know, after all, what it means to say a country or hip-hop or rock performance aired on the show. But no single genre frames the enterprise now. Furthermore, the boundaries between genres are porous ones. I recall watching an *Austin City Limits* set by Susan Tedeschi, who has appeared there several times (Seasons 24, 26, and 29). She covered Stevie Wonder's "Love's In Need of Love Today," Bob Dylan's "Don't Think Twice, It's Alright," and John Prine's "Angel From Montgomery." Musical variety is not new. Any one performance by the late Gatemouth Brown (seasons 2, 3, 5, and 21) moved organically from, say, jazz swing to Texas blues to breakdown fiddle.

The words Terry Lickona used to describe the show on more than one occasion during the past decade include "originality" and "innovation" and "authentic, good music."[30] *Austin City Limits* never respected the vocabulary available to describe its music over the music itself. That made it a great show all along. If the current slogan, "Great Music, No Limits" finally seemed to reconcile content with words, it came only after decades of twists and turns.

During those decades *Austin City Limits* defined and redefined itself against changes in the meaning of Austin and in the meaning of music until what best characterized the show and its home city was openness, a state of readiness to appreciate music from all directions.

Only then could Lickona's words, "original, authentic, good" music, ring true. In some ways, they circle back to those folklorist Archie Green wrote about Austin progressive country: "a pluralistic society, with or without a transcendent national ethos, must find words to mark a people's travel across borders of class, ethnicity, and region."[31] Lickona's words work well to convey the way music crosses borders on *Austin City Limits* today. Yet words alone did not carve out its twenty-first-century identity. *Austin City Limits* expanded in very real, on-the-ground ways as well, specifically in the festival and new venue. Long before then *Austin City Limits* pushed against the margins of commonplace assumptions about what makes music work on television in general, or on PBS in particular.

[6]

A MORE LOVING APPROACH

The Dave Matthews Band kicked off the hour-long opener for Season 35 (2009–2010). Its seven members gave the camera operators plenty of action to shoot. Drummer Carter Beauford alone could hold an audience's attention, moving fluidly around his elaborate kit with multiple toms mounted on a rack, cymbals of every sonic shade (I counted nine), cowbell, woodblock, bar chimes, timbales, and an array of other percussive options. Camera shots during the opening song sometimes change quickly. One, for instance, flows from Beauford's drum fill to a close-up on Boyd Tinsley's violin solo, into another shot that keeps Tinsley in the frame but adds Matthews and guitarist Tim Reynolds to the picture. As Reynolds takes a solo, the camera lingers on his instrument (long enough to learn the chords!), then cuts to the horns, then on to Matthews bopping his head in syncopated approval. The background lights bathe this opening number in blues and whites, and as "Funny the Way It Is" comes to a close the cameras find cheering audience members.

As the performance goes on, the lighting paints its own contours of energy. Blues and whites on the opening song give way to more intense reds and purples by the third. As the set's arguably most intense song, "Squirm," builds toward a peak, the lights build with it, adding yellow, blue, pink, white. They flash excitedly once the song ends, applauding along with the audience. On another song, the lights parallel the background horn accents. During "Sister," they follow more rhythms of the melody but never by rote, never a simplistic one-to-one matchup of color to mood or color to rhythm. Overall the lights construct a sense of progression through each song, and throughout the whole show from its blue/white beginning to the yellow/white that shades the final number.

The second song, "Spaceman," starts more slowly than the first, building an introduction that gives the camera time to dwell on different players in turn. The drums establish the song's mood, then trumpeter Rashawn Ross and saxophonist Jeff Coffin add a layer of long, sustained notes, and, finally, Stefan Lessard lays down the bass lick that underpins the whole tune. Dave Matthews begins to sing and the camera closes in on his expressive face, almost but not precisely at the time his vocals begin. The camera shots move in some sense like a jazz singer—like Billie Holiday or, yes, Willie Nelson—at times with the beat, at times just behind it. Reynolds appends a short guitar solo as a musical postscript to the song, and the camera catches this musical afterthought precisely on time. *Austin City Limits* director Gary Menotti had surely prepped one of the wing camera operators to anticipate it.

Menotti is a master of the "live cut," which in music television refers to the decisions for camera angles and shot sequences made during any given performance. The extent to which the *Austin City Limits* live cut matches the final broadcast is unusual for televised music. Enough cameras roll during a performance to cover any production mistakes in later edits. Nevertheless the final transmission largely comes together during the actual performance. The result feels spontaneous and communicates the energy of live music; modern television rarely captures this vitality outside of game shows, newscasts, and football and other live sports.

Part of the meaning and value of *Austin City Limits* derives from its consistent production quality over time, and expands in proportion to its 40-year history. In this regard the example of the Dave Matthews Band, one of the most commercially successful rock acts of the last two decades, stands out most for *not* standing out among other episodes. With the possible exception of more active lighting appropriate to a so-called stadium act, *Austin City Limits* presents this commercial powerhouse in the same way it presents a performer like Allen Toussaint, a brilliant and solid working musician whose lifelong artistic successes never set *Billboard* chart records. The production team approaches this taping the way it did any others that year: Esperanza Spaulding or Andrew Bird or the Avett Brothers. The end result differs from the live experience, yet derives from and depends upon it. Achieving its live aesthetic entails more than simply pointing a camera in the right direction. It requires an approach that runs counter to television norms.

Televised music in the United States generally follows the structures and demands of commercial television, whose paradigm equates success with "audience share," or the number of sets tuned to a program during any given 15-minute time block.[1] Short, regular, salable blocks of time determine the flow of programming, regardless of whether the program content conforms easily to this arrangement. The flash, the once-in-a-lifetime, the ephemeral all fit pretty well within prescheduled breaks for sponsor advertisements. Though exceptions emerge every now and then, the paradigm leaves little place for substantive encounters with music. It simply is not set up to do so.[2] In the correlation between music and time, the commercial potential of a set unit of time nearly always wins out over the full artistic potential of musical expression.

"Liveness" once typified television but fell away over the years.[3] The clear advantages of prerecording—first on film and then on videotape—gradually squelched widespread live TV.[4] Videotape debuted in the 1960s and gradually established a method "halfway between 'live' and film: *i.e.*, the 'recorded live on video tape' format," which technically describes *Austin City Limits*.[5] Videotape retained the characteristic of immediacy, or "presence," that distinguishes television from film, yet avoided the trapeze-without-a-net aspect of live broadcasting.[6]

At the same time, however, videotape altered TV production practices in ways that work against music on television, never an easy relationship in the first place. Most significantly, multiple takes became the common strategy for increased production quality.[7] Televised performances commonly result from one or two songs repeated multiple times to ensure the best possible camera angles and finished product. Typical television demands a start-and-stop procedure, with the goal of piecing together multiple recordings in the pursuit of visual variety and polished perfection. That can come off well for situation comedy or series drama, with contemporary actors accustomed to repeating a scene over and over. Musicians work differently. It's why Dixie Chicks band member Martie McGuire declared TV the worst possible venue for musicians.[8] While the end result might be polished and smooth, these circumstances suck away the vitality.

A live concert creates an arc with a beginning, middle, and end, characterized by spontaneity and interchange with the audience in the room. Multiple takes make studio audiences uncomfortable. Multiple takes counteract television's immediacy and, therefore, undermine the potency of live music. Repetition, heavy editing, and often audio overdubbing (or even lip-syncing in some cases), all of which serve the needs of television, stultify the energy and

Figure 6.1 During a panel moderated by Lauren Onkey, vice president of Education and Public Programs at the Rock and Roll Hall of Fame, Martie McGuire talks about *Austin City Limits* with other panelists. From right to left: Onkey; Emily Robison, sister of McGuire and one-third of the Dixie Chicks trio; McGuire; Terry Lickona; Alejandro Escovedo; Jim Henke, then curator of the Rock and Roll Hall of Fame.

flow for musicians. These practices facilitate technically based, artificially realized craft, but also carve away or usurp the musical vigor of live performance. In short, they kill the muse.

Austin City Limits avoids these problems by stepping outside televisual norms to tape an actual, uninterrupted live performance before a receptive audience. The live aesthetic stands out because the circumstances of its production are more authentic than most other televised music. Time is the key—a singular precondition for the muse to appear. The fact that *Austin City Limits* gives primacy to music (or the muse) shores up its authenticity and its live aesthetic, and distinguishes it from other ongoing music broadcasts.

Bill Arhos knew this when he responded to a viewer in 1983 that "we're still one of a very few television series that is most like a live concert and we can extend that experience to the whole country. Willie Nelson looked ridiculous on 'Saturday Night Live' because he only got to do two songs 30 minutes apart. Given a half hour he becomes the 'monster' musician, vocalist, songwriter that he really is."[9] *Austin City Limits* gives 30-minute or full-hour performances to every artist, in contrast with most other musical television, including performances on morning or late-night talk shows. The performance is primary for everyone involved.

Musicians often remark on how unusual the whole experience taping *Austin City Limits* is when compared to other television performances. Texas singer-songwriter Robert Earl Keen once told a reporter, " 'It's absolutely the finest music show you can be on as an artist.... You have creative control. No one tells you your songs are too long or too short, or asks you if you can fill this time slot. You can get the chance to just do your show.' "[10] In an after-show interview with *Austin City Limits* staff member Laura Bond in 1995, blues legend B.B. King reflected:

This is one of the few times in my whole career that I felt very comfortable doing a television show and not paying any attention to it. Tonight, it was like I was on stage, just playing. It was more like my show. It really was—I felt like I was just doing my show on stage. It was hot to us—the energy was there for us, there was plenty of energy. If the cameras saw it that way, then that's OK.[11]

Austin City Limits asks performers to put on a concert for a live audience and lets its team convey that performance as best they can. They take what Terry Lickona describes "as a more deliberate, a more loving approach to the way we capture the performance with the emphasis being on the performance not so much the direction or the director's style."[12] Then cameraman Doug Robb made it sound simple enough when he talked after The Decemberists 2007 taping: "We try to create an environment for the musicians where they can come in and do their show the way they do it with their regular instrumentation, their regular stage setup, and we just are there to document it. We try to not influence it as much as possible." Artists do not get asked to repeat a song because the cameras failed to get their angle, or an audience member got in the way of a shot. I have seen performers themselves repeat a song they felt went poorly. Chan Marshall, better known as Cat Power, started and stopped her acoustic version of "House of the Rising Sun" at least seven times because she never got the right feel.[13] Regardless, staff members do their best to stay out of the way.

This holds true even when in-house technical glitches ruin a shot. Jeff Bridges, for example, taped an episode in the Moody Theater for Season 37. His band, The Abiders, assembled with the help of his producer, T-Bone Burnett, included Carrie Rodriguez as a vocalist and sometimes fiddler. One-time Austin fixture Augie Meyers joined them as well, later confessing that he heard the songs for the first time during rehearsal. A technical malfunction of the atmospheric, light-enhancing "fog" machine created more haze than normal. It bordered on being too thick—Menotti kept calling it barbecue smoke—and all agreed to kill the haze altogether. The skyline backdrop was having issues too. It kept blinking on and off in the middle of a song and no one could figure out why. It happened during one song and Menotti said, "I can't save that one," meaning that he could not hide the problem by changing the camera shot during editing. It was a relief then when Bridges called for his band to do the song again. In the end, Bridges, a movie star accustomed to cameras and multiple takes, called for repeating five out of his 14 songs.

For the most part musicians taping for *Austin City Limits* gradually forget about the cameras and realize they can play their show. As David Hough recalled,

> When we finally got Johnny Cash, his experience with television in Nashville was horrible, and the description was "stop-and-go television," doing things again.... He finally relaxed after the second song. I see that with a lot of bands. They fall into the comfort zone. We have five or six cameras going, and one trick we use is to tape over the tally light so that they don't know which camera is on. They play to the audience and the audience gives the energy back to the band. The whole idea of the show is to give the home viewer some semblance of what the experience would be like if they were in the studio.[14]

Historically speaking music and television met on uneasy terms from the start, and never really worked out their relationship. Beginning slowly in the 1930s, a story interrupted by World War II, television seeped into national consciousness in the United States. No one doubted that the medium changed the experience of music. Likewise no one seemed clear on what to do with that knowledge. Writers imagined the new technology innovating relationships between the visible and the audible. Some early published pieces take on the same bemusing ring as late nineteenth-century predictions about the phonograph and how it would streamline stenographers' work in business, or about the radio and how its lack of privacy would impede its usefulness.[15] Other writers foresaw developments that, in one form or another, came to fruition as music videos or, later, in the form of the iTunes Visualizer.[16]

After the war music and industry trade magazines began debating the relative merits versus constraints of "audiovisuals" on both artistry and musician–audience communication.[17] Just as it would for politics, television changed the playing field for musicians. Arturo Toscanini's more flamboyant conducting style went over far more effectively on screen than the relatively constrained baton work of Eugene Ormandy.[18] Likewise, a visually exciting bandleader like Cab Calloway found himself in great demand for early television broadcasts. Toscanini and Calloway added pizzazz to the otherwise problematically mundane sight of musicians playing their instruments. The associate producer for the live big-band performance show *Cavalcade of Bands* gave advice in *Downbeat* magazine about the special demands for musicians on television in 1951: "there must be plenty of sections playing since the cameras have to keep changing pace to maintain audience interest."[19]

As television developed, music there suffered a malady similar to that which frustrated Pierre Bourdieu when he considered how the medium handles news: it makes the extraordinary mundane and the everyday sensational. The same often goes for music, which on television either gets sensationalized to the point of absurdity (e.g., Madonna on the 2012 Super Bowl halftime show dressed in a gold-and-black getup that alternately evoked Vikings, Roman soldiers, and high school cheerleaders) or distanced to the point that even the most compelling performance seems of little consequence (e.g., late-night talk shows that squeeze artists in between back-slapping repartee by the host, plugs to buy an upcoming release, and foretastes of the next guest coming on after the commercial break).

Musical broadcasts over the course of television history have tended toward one or the other side of a spectrum: spectacle at this end and humdrum at that. A fascination with the "spectacular" finds its roots all the way back in early film.[20] Beginning with instrumental scores for silent movies and early films like *The Jazz Singer*, the idea of pairing popular songs with enthralling images took hold. The mid-1960s Beatles film *A Hard Day's Night* was a linchpin in the story because it introduced a new way to conceive music's relationship to images.[21] Afterward savvy musicians and television business people began to understand both film and TV anew. Both media offered a means to create, package, and market visualized music as cultural products for consumers, and this dynamic reached its peak with MTV, VH1, and other television outlets during the 1980s.[22] There, on the cable channels that seemed so fresh an alternative to broadcast, music videos brought the complex adornment of early Hollywood musicals to bear on slick late-twentieth-century production values, resulting in production shorts like Michael Jackson's "Thriller" and Peter Gabriel's "Sledgehammer."

At the opposite end of spectacle comes the treatment of music on television as a poor substitute for being there: point a camera or two and shoot.[23] With rare exceptions like the 2009 movie version of Puccini's *La Bohème*, directed by Robert Dornhelm and broadcast on PBS, opera tends to be filmed in this spirit for television broadcasts. In most cases the approach amounts to a self-fulfilling prophecy, and the results are an inadequate stand-in for live experience. Despite technological leaps in digital fidelity like Dolby 5.1 and home theater capability, visual still trumps audio in the overall hierarchy of television priorities.[24]

Along this continuum of over- or underdone musical television, *Austin City Limits* occupies a middle ground. It avoids the flash that typifies contemporary televised music ranging from ubiquitous videos to award events like the Country Music Association annual broadcast. There, for instance, a Little Big Town performance in 2012 positioned the performers on raised platform compartments, surrounded by explosions of color, light, and text. If scholar Raymond Williams defined sensationalism at its extreme as "the isolation of an experience from its context, and then its dramatic exploitation," then that explains why Little Big Town seemed simultaneously sensational and remote—an anomaly on the living room screen.[25]

It also partly accounts for what makes *Austin City Limits* work on that very same screen. Up close and personal, *Austin City Limits* portrays the embodied nature of musical performance and the emotional immediacy of live music in an apparently straightforward fashion. Yet the facility of the end results obscures the depth of technical achievement. In a way akin to how a makeup artist creates a "natural" sense of beauty via a mix of intuitive artistry and sophisticated technique, *Austin City Limits* conveys a realistic presentation of musical performance.[26] The portrayal is "unglossed," communicating respect for musical artistry and concern for musical integrity, but it also fills vacancies that mediation confers upon live performance. In short, watching the show feels less like a faint echo of the live musical experience, and more like an altogether different encounter with music through the screen.

Austin City Limits is unrealistic, if realism means the precise correlation between musical proceedings and televised transmission. Television cuts break that continuity. For example, at one point during the Dave Matthews Band concert, a moment cut in post-production edits, the singer must have changed off screen from a six-string acoustic to a twelve-string electric guitar. More to the point, the cameras make possible multiple frames of reference, showing television audiences a view not possible for a person present in the room.[27] For cameraman Doug Robb this aspect makes the televised experience superior in some ways to the live one since the studio audience takes in the show "always in the same frame of reference."[28] In that sense viewers get a more "full concert experience, as if you were in different seats simultaneously in the house." At another moment, for example, we do see Dave Matthews switch guitars, but we see it through a wide overhead shot from up high, 45 degrees or so stage right, with audience, band, and the approximate Austin cityscape all in the frame at once.

Furthermore, camera operators do more than capture performers in action. They also craft what Menotti calls "beauty shots." Cameraman Robert Moorhead hunts these shots with either the handheld camera or one of the "jibs," or smaller crane cameras. Beauty shots often include "either some kind of set piece or using the audience as a set piece."[29] It could be a simple close-up of hands clapping with other audience members visible in the background. Or it might present a perspective completely impossible except through the camera lens. Moorhead recalled one memorable shot through a clear drumhead so that viewers "see the drummer's face...through the drumhead that he's hitting." These shots have "more to do with adding to the atmosphere" than conveying the progress of the music. They are one way the production crew uses tools of the medium to create something new from the possibilities that emanate from any performance.

The television camera lenses also guide the viewer in and around intricacies of the performance, taking care to explain what might not be self-evident. So, for example, when Jeff Coffin coaxes an unusual, winding, almost buzzing effect (a Turkish zurna comes to mind) on his baritone sax during "Squirm," the cameras respond to an unspoken question and show him. Other questions get answered before they are asked. Where is that sound coming from? We get a good look at the shiny silver guitar slide Reynolds wears on his pinky for a particular lick from "Lying in the Hands of God." How do band members interact? How do the performers relate to the song? To the audience? Dave Matthews fist bumps one band member just as a song ends. We see the look of joy on Beauford's face and Coffin blowing with great concentration into his soprano saxophone, weaving notes up and down the tune. We see Dave Matthews's neckline, up close from behind, and the audience before him just as he sees it during this performance. Carter Beauford blows a bubble with his chewing gum, a goofy kind of counterpoint to all the layers of groove he creates with his every limb—one the studio audience likely missed.

If the view of live musical performance on *Austin City Limits* is unrealistic in some sense, it is also hyper-realistic in ways that compensate for the loss of physical energy or "aura" that television cannot transfer.[30] This works especially well on *Austin City Limits* given the show's emphasis on popular genres. While orchestral or jazz performers tend to downplay outward demonstrations of emotion, the display of emotional immediacy and intensity are critical performance conventions for many pop music styles. In other words, the power of popular music stems in part from the flesh and blood of its performers and the embodied response of its listeners. *Austin City Limits,* in this regard, uses television's customary close-up camera shots to underscore the physicality of a performance: the deep dimple that cuts a musician's cheek, the sweat on a guitar player's brow, the way a singer's eyes sweep over the audience. These hyper-realistic elements fill the gaps of not being there with insights available only through the camera lens. Something new results.

The power of live music inspired *Austin City Limits*. Its audience in the studio and its audience on television both encounter that power, but not in the same way. The TV experience differs from the live experience. At the same time, the live experience determines what airs on TV. Grasping that the relationship between the live and the televised experience is related but not the same in part explains why *Austin City Limits* has no lasting contenders. Communicating the crux of the total musical experience eludes more televised music productions than not.

During the Dave Matthews Band episode the audience–performer "vibe" builds on screen over time. As the band moves deeper into the set, we see more shots of audience members getting into the music, dancing or singing the lyrics. These kinds of shots, emphasized even more in recent seasons, "bring a certain amount of that aliveness," as Moorhead put it, and show "there really is an audience, these people really are having fun." Equally important are "shots of the artist interacting with the audience." In this case, Matthews speaks for the first time when he introduces "Squirm" as "a love song of sorts." He later deadpans his appreciation for the audience joining him "outside" before Austin's twinkling skyline. Before the last song Matthews describes how the band collectively worked the song "Why I Am" out of a sense of chaos and frustration, and he dedicates it to departed friend and band member LeRoi Moore. As the tune nears its end, the camera pans across to take in all the band members from one side to the other, keeping Matthews at center all the while.

For *Austin City Limits* the live aesthetic shapes the production much more than the production shapes the live aesthetic. Yet the show does more than transmit the live event. *Austin City Limits* people grasp the unique and powerful way that television conveys "the close and observable connection between the source of the message and the experience being communicated."[31] That sounds intuitive enough. Yet achieving that connection is hard to pin down when it comes to music because the experience itself proves elusive. Musical performance entails so many unutterable aspects. *Austin City Limits* uses camera angles and edits to do more than infuse atmosphere or construct distinctive views. It portrays insights into the music-making uniquely accessible through the broadcast. The end results distinguish *Austin City Limits* as a televised music performance program. Within the United States PBS is the only media context where *Austin City Limits* could do what it does so well, and for so long.

[7]

WE'RE NOT ELITIST, WE'VE GOT *AUSTIN CITY LIMITS*

Surfing the Internet for *Austin City Limits* on a mid-October afternoon in 2012, you might have visited acltv.com. This site includes a link to station KLRU's website that, in turn, posts four full episodes on a monthly rotating schedule, plus 79 "previews" and 75 "shorts" from recent broadcasts. It would take 16 ½ hours to watch all the content posted there from start to finish, but no one thinks you will. Your interest in the television program led you, as its Web designers hoped, to digital content that allows you to explore episodes you missed on the scheduled local PBS airing.

You click on the clip of Tom Waits performing in Season 4, one of the most iconic of all *Austin City Limits* episodes, first broadcast back in 1979 and re-aired as a special "encore" on Christmas Eve 2011. Your Twitter feed, along with Facebook, had mentioned this episode showing as a "Reel Rarity" at Austin's Alamo Drafthouse cinema, an event that raised funds for the Health Alliance for Austin Musicians (HAAM). Here at your laptop, far from Austin and even farther from 1979, you dwell temporarily in a meaningful and mediated intersection of time, space, place, and music for the 5 minutes and 46 seconds it takes to stream the excerpt.

You are experiencing modern (what was once known as) television. You encounter *Austin City Limits* as a mediated entity in this age of digital "convergence"[1] with Tom Waits himself, the program's history and critical reputation, its production style, its link to the city of Austin, and its presence on PBS as ingredients in the mix. And you feel yourself transported from your immediate surroundings for nearly six minutes, the time it took Tom Waits to perform "Christmas Card from a Hooker in Minneapolis," off the album *Blue Valentine,* on a night three decades ago in Texas.

As the song starts, the cameras begin from up high with the pianist, the bass player, and a portion of the drum set in the shot. The frame is just wide enough to capture the drummer's hands "tinking" the triangle, the only occasional accompaniment to Waits's piano and his half-spoken, half-sung lyrics addressed to "Charlie." The camera lingers on the performer's face, showing enough of his hands to convey their motion over the keyboard.

Then the shot looks toward him from the end of the piano, with the instrument's inner workings exposed to show the hammers lift and lower as Waits works the damper pedal. The camera gradually narrows toward his face and head, both in constant motion, until a cross fade moves to a side angle as the phrase ends. The bass player listens meditatively in the background, arms wrapped around the instrument, with Waits's hands now fully visible. Maybe this is one of those views director Menotti would call a beauty shot. From this angle, the light catches the deep shadow of Waits's dimple as he smiles at a line that draws laughter from the audience ("I still think about you, man, every time I pass a filling station [pause] on account of all the grease you used to wear in your hair").

As Waits sets off deeper into the vignette, shots vary to show the performer from overhead, coming in from behind, now with the keyboard and his left hand fully in view, and the drummer partially in the frame. We linger on an up-close front view of his face as the song emotionally intensifies, and we remain there through a line that injects one last fleeting touch of humor. As Waits sings the ending to a mostly spoken verse, the camera shot cuts quickly to a side view, showing both singer and instrument. It comes just in time for the more melodically active piano lick that propels toward the song's peak when the protagonist reveals that her message so far to Charlie has been largely false: she doesn't really have a husband, may or may not be pregnant, and is, in fact, desperate, writing from jail, and in need of some cash.

A quicker front-to-side camera cut mirrors the increased musical, narrative, and stylistic motion as Waits brings the song to its poignant end. Unlike the album version, he ends this performance just like he opened it, with an off-kilter quotation of the Christmas hymn "Silent Night." The camera zeroes in on his hands for a couple of lines, then a front view of his face, until it fades back to an overhead shot from the left side, bringing some studio audience into the frame as Waits delivers the last phrase. The cameras have taken the television audience from a bird's-eye view of the room to an intimate, inside experience of the performance, and then back out again.

No other television outlet in the United States would have aired an hour-long Tom Waits performance except for PBS. In 1979 on *Austin City Limits* Waits joined a salmagundi lineup alongside other Season 4 artists like Taj Mahal, Tom T. Hall, and Marcia Ball. Some things remain constant. Thirty years later, Season 35 throws the Dave Matthews Band and Allen Toussaint in with Madeleine Peyroux, Asleep at the Wheel, Willie Nelson (making his fourteenth appearance on the show), Mos Def and Kenny Chesney, St. Vincent and K'Naan, Pearl Jam, and so on. Lineups like these run counter to commercial TV logic, and within this logic *Austin City Limits* would not have survived.

Commercial television producers need to hit immediately and steadily to stay on the air. Advertisers spend huge amounts of money to put their products before a relevant and receptive audience, which needs a predictable, measurable, and sustainable demography to justify the expense. This situation has produced some compelling, significant moments on the small screen, but the system does not bear risk very well.[2] More shows get cancelled than not, which explains why television programs in general, not just musical ones, tend toward either of two options. They play it safe, with bland, formulaic fare that often mirrors already-existing successful shows.[3] Or they play it sensational. Television events like the Super Bowl or the Olympics are intensely hyped for the promise of a one-time rather than ongoing audience draw. Special episodes or guest appearances for series, particularly during "sweeps" periods when Nielsen ratings come in, operate by a similar strategy.[4] For all its pleasures and achievements, the short-cycle economics of most commercial television could not bear the ups and downs of a decades-long concert program that is neither safe nor sensational, with ambiguous demographics, regardless of how consistent its high standard of production or artistically compelling its shows.

The situation gets more and more pronounced. In an environment of exponential media channels, demographics drive the trend toward "narrowcasting" as a tactic for financial survival on commercial TV.[5] In its early days MTV, for example, aimed toward a very specific segment of viewers. Now channels focus solely on particular interests like shopping or cooking or home improvement. Channels devoted to sports continue subdividing like red blood cells into channels for golf, soccer, basketball, football,

NASCAR, horseracing, skiing, and so on. Again, commercial television makes no room for a series program whose targeted demographic group is fuzzy in terms of age or race or education or any of the parameters that inform most program schedules. How could advertisers know whom they were reaching with a lineup like Season 35, or any other for that matter?

PBS not only positioned *Austin City Limits* to weather the erratic winds of commercial culture, to experiment with content, and to explore new directions. It shaped the program's identity in other ways, too—*Austin City Limits* derives a distinct ambiance from its noncommercial PBS context. Any television presentation carries more weight in the absence of interruptive advertisements. Major presidential speeches and debates, for instance, avoid them even on the private networks. The lack of commercials on public broadcasting programs conveys a more pronounced sense of gravitas than on their private counterparts.[6]

This quality mattered especially for *Austin City Limits* when it first began. At the time no one else presented country music—progressive or mainstream—"in a serious vein."[7] As photographer Scott Newton put it, "On the commercial TV you had *Hee Haw* but, you know, in between every song they're selling you dog food. You know, we could have Willie Nelson and there's no dog food. And we could project the art as what it was, the music of the people, you know, the real pop music." PBS legitimized and grounded the contents of *Austin City Limits*. It imparted a tone of respectability.

On the flip side, *Austin City Limits* meant just as much to the identity of PBS. The show arguably altered the trajectory of US public broadcasting. For one thing, coming as it did "not far after the whole freaking invention of public television," to quote the estimable words of Vice President for Brand Development Ed Bailey,[8] *Austin City Limits* helped loosen the girdle on "culture" as defined by PBS programs up to that point. Music programming during early PBS years tended toward orchestral styles, or so-called "serious" music. *Austin City Limits* was at the vanguard for a kind of musical programming audiences now expect to see there: a retrospective documentary on Johnny Cash, a Fleetwood Mac reunion concert, or a diachronic history of rock-and-roll. In this regard, the program pushed PBS to expand its breadth of programming and, in so doing, its audience.[9]

More significantly, the show came to represent fulfillment of the founding mission for public broadcasting, serving as both symbol and sign for the innovation, widespread relevance, and reflection of diversity toward which PBS presumably aspired. High ideals over a half-century old still guide public broadcasting today, as PBS touts its mission to produce television that "educates, informs, and inspires."[10] Those ideals first took shape at the outmost edges of the broadcasting industry.

In contrast to most countries, where public or state-run television developed and then private stations followed, the commercial networks came first and established the industry's norms in the United States. These norms sprouted from the infrastructure and business models put in place by the powerful radio networks during the late 1920s and early 1930s. The "big three" (ABC, NBC, and CBS) set the terms for radio and, in turn, television operation. Public television came along as something of an afterthought, and emerged in the United States as an alternative to mainstream broadcasting rather than an integral part of it.

Public television broadcasting first surfaced in 1952 when the FCC reserved channels for noncommercial "educational" stations (ETV). The commission reasoned that broadcast airwaves were a limited "public good," like highways or water, not to be left entirely to the quicksilver ways of commerce.[11] These educational channels clustered at one end of the broadcast spectrum, a practical manifestation of public service broadcasting's dwelling place at the ideological and economic margins of the wider industry.

Two notions slowly but surely pushed public television forward. The first was that of unrealized potential. When FCC Chair Newton Minow famously characterized television programming as a "vast wasteland" in 1961, he asserted the limitations of the commercial television paradigm. Minow pegged commercial networks as reluctant to take the risks necessary for innovation, to explore possibilities for airwaves bringing science, nature, history, politics, and the arts to citizens in every corner of the nation. He argued that measures for broadcasting success should expand beyond short-term sales figures. His thinking parallels a similar democratic impulse that, once upon a time, pushed yellow journalism aside for news reporting standards of balance and equal time.[12] The commercial system, Minow asserted, effectively stifles programming, discouraging ventures into unexplored possibilities for the medium.

The second notion drew on democratic ideals of representation and applied them to program creation. In order to reflect and serve the widely diverse US population effectively, television programming should originate from across the country. These principles moved a step closer to action in 1967 when Lyndon B. Johnson signed the Public Broadcasting Act, a congressional amendment to the 1934 Communications Act.[13] This legislation set up the Corporation for Public Broadcasting (CPB) as a structure of private and public funds to help support programming, a long-missing piece of the financial puzzle for public television operators. Beginning two years later the Public Broadcasting Service (PBS) linked stations to improve proficiency in program distribution while at the same time maintaining their independence. In signing the act, Johnson said, "Every region and community should be challenged to contribute its best."[14] Together the CPB and PBS, then, specifically aimed to support television production outside the established centers of Hollywood and New York City.

Austin City Limits realized the ideals of public broadcasting in practice. During its early years the show's creators pushed the tenet of local, regional productions as a central point of persuasion. A mid-1970s *Austin City Limits* press release states that PBS, in contrast with commercial TV, has "both the sensitivity to recognize such community/regional developments [such as the flowering of progressive country] as well as the flexibility to document them as they occur for national appreciation."[15] Later *Austin City Limits* took on further import as counter-evidence against charges of PBS's elitism.[16] A series renewal proposal for Season 19 (1993), for example, first cites the public television goal to "honor our commitment to serve all Americans," then states that *Austin City Limits* "is *foremost* among PBS series in attracting viewers with a high school equivalency or less with that category representing approximately 75% of *Austin City Limits* viewers.... This set of demographics is significant in refuting the charges of 'elitism' frequently hurled at the system."[17] Even more to the point, *Austin American-Statesman* reporter Diane Holloway quoted a speech a few years later by then PBS president Ervin Duggan, who "responded to charges that the network is elitist by declaring, 'We're not elitist. We've got 'Austin City Limits.' "[18]

"Elite versus populist" rings familiar alongside other recurring tropes in debates about US television. More often than not talk about public and private broadcasting positions the two in conflict with noncommercial on one side and commercial on the other: service versus sales; art versus commerce.[19] Yet a stark public/private split never strictly characterized broadcasting in the United

States, at least since Nixon vetoed congressional funding in 1972. Corporate sponsorship has fueled PBS programming ever since.[20] Like other PBS programs, *Austin City Limits* always depended to some degree on underwriters, companies that financially support the program in exchange for mention at its start and finish. This reality makes it impossible to talk of private and public, or commercial and service broadcasting, in rigid black-and-white terms in the United States.[21]

Product sales and marketing strategies constitute another gray area. A documentary from the PBS *American Experience* history series, for example, offers online links to a summary and timeline for the topic, bibliography, teachers' guides and other supporting materials, as well as a place to purchase the documentary itself, with proceeds divided between the series and PBS.[22] *Austin City Limits* DVDs and CDs, produced through an agreement with New West Records, sell to home viewers via the "shoppbs.org" website alongside products related to other PBS programs. At one point in the late 1990s *Austin City Limits* distributed its press kits in a "large perforated-board envelope" with facts about the Indigo Girls or other performers on punch-out "collector cards."[23]

In other words, sponsorship money matters both for US public and private broadcasters, but in different ways. Profit, particularly the potential for it in every isolated time unit, drives commercial television programming in a singular way that often pushes aside other measures of value. Public television sponsors buy into a longer-term association with quality, sincerity, and discernment that characterize public broadcasting more generally.[24] Not that they don't expect a positive return on their financial investment, but they measure it in less clear cut ways than last quarter's dividends. In the case of an ongoing series like *Austin City Limits,* program sponsors do not expect input regarding programming decisions because the paradigm excludes that type of role. As Terry Lickona put it, "Underwriters would not think to bring it up."[25]

Demographics also matter for public and commercial broadcasters. For *Austin City Limits* the audience makeup has periodically factored into the history of charting directions for the show. As the 1980s ended and a transition seemed inevitable, KLRU station management deliberately pushed to lower viewer demographics from the 50-plus to the 18–49 age category.[26] During the 1990s PBS stepped up pressure for *Austin City Limits* "to reach a wider audience,"[27] and a newspaper article reported that around 49 percent of the show's TV audience was in the 18–49 category, 50 percent was still over fifty, and "only 1 percent are under 18." Arhos mused that "we tried to attract more young people by presenting younger artists and our older viewership just went up more."[28]

During the 1990s the word "brand," which is linked closely with demographics, took hold within the entire broadcasting industry. The term had migrated over time from its original application to tangible commodities such as a pair of jeans, a soda, or a box of facial tissues to broader, more amorphous entities like a network, a rock band, a university, or even a city. Disney introduced the term to broadcasting parlance during the 1950s, fully exploiting and embracing its commercial implications.[29] And the mid-1990s fervor for "re-branding" among major networks has been pegged to the quick rise of cable television, as a response to diminishing audiences.[30] PBS, too, began to conceive of itself in these terms, hiring "an advertising agency to revamp its 'brand' image" in 1995.[31]

Branding public television may seem like an infiltration—a sign of cheapening or degradation of every aspect of life to the level of commodity. Yet US public broadcasting was never naive to the concerns of its commercial predecessors. Both public and private broadcasters share interests in service and financial viability, each according to distinct strategies for prioritizing and addressing those concerns. A "brand" proposes a flexible, value-laden structure of meaning. It explains how or why a person might come to love and identify with a public television show or a college or Shakespeare, a game show or a corner fast-food spot or a cheesy romance novel. "Brand" accounts for why *Austin City Limits* invites metaphors like the musical "Good Housekeeping Seal of Approval,"[32] or why country rocker Miranda Lambert, relatively unknown at the time outside her native Texas when she taped a show for the 2005–2006 season, paused in her faded jeans and Merle Haggard "The Hag" T-shirt to gush to the studio audience, "Now I know I have arrived."[33] The notion of the "brand" also explains how *Austin City Limits* and *Great Performances at the Met* might draw the same viewer to PBS.[34]

Branding, especially as a breezy shorthand for cultural capital, means more now than it did in the late 1990s. Among broadcasters the "re-branding" impulse continues, driven by the "instability," competition, and "clutter" of the Internet.[35] In other words, branding is more and more merely a strategy for getting attention in an information-saturated world. Internet streaming and related practices constitute a shake-up to the television and popular music industries that parallels the technology-driven upheaval of the mid-1950s.[36] Gigabyte clouds and handheld devices radically change the way we experience television. People don't wait for their favorite show to air at a scheduled time each week so much as they seek the programs they want to watch via the Internet and view them when they wish. This means that Nielsen ratings no longer account for success even in commercial terms since audiences "experience" a show far outside the temporal bounds of its weekly broadcast.[37]

The challenge for audiences in relation to ever-propagating media content is to make choices. As media scholar William Uricchio suggests, "the overwhelming mass of information available in general increases the need for trustworthy editorial services."[38] These services take any number of forms. They come via one of the narrowcasting networks geared toward people who like history, or classic movies, news, or reality shows.[39] They come through so-called third-party services like Pandora, Spotify, Last.fm, the suggestions Netflix generates based on viewing patterns, or programmable devices that map choices based on input preferences.[40]

Thanks to its brand *ACL* can act as its own filter among these too-many choices. In its design *Austin City Limits* already fits well with the fragmented attention generally attributed to television audiences.[41] The popular song format, shorter by nature than, say, a Beethoven symphony, suits the Web even more dramatically than it does terrestrial TV. On the latter *Austin City Limits* lends itself to aesthetic continuity even if a television audience member leaves the room or temporarily becomes distracted.[42] The end of one song and the beginning of another is a ready-made moment of transition. For that same reason an *Austin City Limits* broadcast divides readily into short segments that can be watched online during small windows of downtime on the computer. Incidentally, the program is the PBS website's most regularly streamed content.

A Google search for "Tom Waits" on a November afternoon in 2012 brings 28,800,000 hits. When you narrow it down to "Tom Waits performance" 5,010,000 possibilities still pop up. Sampling every one is not among the possible strategies for making a choice. But the one from *Austin City Limits* catches your eye. Amid the contemporary fragmented media environment *Austin City Limits* offers the sense of orientation and context that aesthetic pleasure requires. For the 5-minute-and-46-second segment of Tom Waits performing in 1979 you experience something as extraordinary as it is widely accessible. You step outside the mundane routine of everyday life to become immersed in a powerful musical moment. The aesthetic experience comes from more than a great performance, although that is part of it. The experience is intimately bound up with all the cultural capital that *Austin City Limits* communicates. Its production style, PBS home, and geographic grounding are aspects of the context that make *Austin City Limits* a meaningful experience, whether encountered as an episode watched on Friday night television or a clip viewed on the computer screen during a midday lunch break.

Once a weekly hour-long PBS program, *Austin City Limits* now sustains a multifaceted identity as a broadcast program with a live aesthetic and a movable, repeatable, transferrable commodity that can exist as a DVD or as a web stream to be watched any time of day or night, via computer or game system or handheld device. *Austin City Limits* circulates now on the level of ideas, and as an idea—a brand, if you prefer—it potentially structures the experience of meaning and aesthetic pleasure for its audience. The intellectual reset that occurred somewhere around the milestone twenty-fifth anniversary repositioned *Austin City Limits* for dramatic changes to come with the new century.

[8]

DON'T MOVE HERE

The ground feels like a mud facial or, where any grass remains, a wet sponge. Near the back of the crowd gathered for Sunday afternoon's set by the B-52s, I smell a combination of cigarette smoke, truck-stop bathroom, wet hay, and kettle corn. The festival sights are more mud-splattered than normal today, but familiar nonetheless: people spread out on chairs and blankets, colorful flags and balloons rising high from sticks planted here and there, a beach ball bouncing its way back and forth across the crowd, a beer can resting in hand after hand. It is an exercise in focused listening, easy to drift away from the B-52s singing "Rock Lobster" toward the conversation among the cluster of middle-aged men passing around a camera for group photos. The booming and beats from the stage across the way create a thumping, incongruous counterpoint to the "red snappers snappin' and the clam shells clappin'" from the stage ahead. Looking around, people move across the field at Zilker Park like ocean water, in waves.

Senses can get overloaded here: bodies jostling together, sounds mingling from different musical acts, the sight of a woman in a flowing, white, gauzy dress smeared brown with mud to her waist, feet bare, eyes closed, dancing even when the music stops. Senses can also get deprived. The lines for food extend at least 50 people deep at peak hunger times, and sometimes it seems best to put off eating rather than miss the music. The bathroom situation is so daunting—slow-moving, no toilet paper, filthy—that it's best not to drink to avoid a trip there. Exhaustion from last night's late return, following an hour-and-a-half wait for a 15-minute shuttle ride back to downtown Austin's Republic Square, adds a hazy tinge to the entire experience. And yet the *Austin City Limits* Music Festival appeals to its audience at a level beyond the regular five senses. It appeals to other, deeper senses—a sense of connectedness and a sense of "being there."

Looking toward downtown Austin from the middle of Zilker Park, the city skyline spreads across the horizon. The sight links this moment visually to the PBS television show that lends the festival its name. On TV plywood and Christmas lights long created

Figure 8.1 The *ACL* Music Festival crowd remained undaunted by the rain during *ACL* 2009.

the illusion, one that changed only a little between 1982 and 2011 when the new venue opened with an updated rendering of downtown. For Lisa Hickey, marketing director for the company that stages the festival, the music at Zilker Park unfolds "underneath the *real* Austin skyline—that's what we like to say." She recalls the mystique of the television show in her younger years: "I guess I was even in high school wondering where that venue was that they taped *Austin City Limits*—'they have a great view of downtown'—and it took me forever before I realized it was a studio."[1]

For decades the plywood skyline communicated the idea of Austin as a musical city. People both within and without Austin's city limits believed the idea, built upon it with care and deliberation, and made it so. In light of Austin's musical history over the past few decades, it seems fair to ask which skyline is more real. People attend the *ACL* Music Festival to experience Austin, which they do in tangible ways, from the dry, warm air they breathe to the scoop of locally made Amy's Ice Cream served at the "Austin Eats Food Court." People likewise come for the idea of Austin, as a hip town with an authentically vital musical life. The idea holds as much power as the lived experience, and perhaps the two cannot be separated in the end. The guy behind the Hudson's On the Bend booth must have recognized that with some wariness as he dished out a taste of Austin to some of the 75,000 people attending the festival that weekend. As he put a "Hot 'n' Crunchy Chicken Cone" in my hand, I noted the message scrawled in thick, black magic marker on his plain white T-shirt: "Don't Move Here."[2]

The *ACL* Music Festival promises an experience. The depth of that experience springs from its unique intersection of tangible and symbolic realms: the physical discipline and real-life material encounter with the history, identity, and idea or brand of *Austin City Limits,* and all that contains. From the start both the city itself

Figure 8.2 The entrance gate for the *ACL* Music Festival, shown here in 2009, promises a powerful experience.

and the long history of its best-known media export, *Austin City Limits,* anchored the festival and in that way it stands out among other events of its kind.[3] No other festival shares a television show with the same name. Likewise no other festival draws on the "long history, the track record, the reputation, credibility, and the relationship with artists that *Austin City Limits* the TV show has built and nurtured so carefully all these decades."[4] All that together amounted to something akin to instant cachet. That may account for the festival's rapid success, something no one involved anticipated.

When the *ACL* Music Festival began it merged two very different aesthetic enterprises: the intimate, highly mediated televised concert associated with folk music and the outdoor festival of a scale associated with rock. In some ways the festival seems

Figure 8.3 At peak temperatures, festival participants cluster for a bite to eat or just to relax under one of the grounds' precious shade trees.

antithetical to the TV show. The intimacy, the sense of musical focus, and the sound quality that distinguishes *Austin City Limits* on television do not apply at the festival. The festival seems more like a Roman spectacle or an eighteenth-century opera: people come to eat and drink and talk with their companions. The musical sound itself is auxiliary. The video projections of any given performance-in-progress onto giant screens framing each large festival stage do not demand the same artful, unobtrusive camera angles that typify the televisual style of *Austin City Limits*.

Likewise time precludes the careful sound craft that has shaped the audio for every *Austin City Limits* episode since the pilot. At the festival its quality varies stage by stage. In 2009 whoever operated the board for the Xbox 360 stage achieved a more balanced mix than on the AMD stage across the field. There, driving bass vibrations through the bones of everyone within 500 feet took precedence over hearing John Legend's voice. Nevertheless energy builds throughout the crowd. Legend's voice hovers just above its reach, as he sings out Bob Marley's "Redemption Song." This moment crystallizes around that shared sense of "being there," and extends far beyond the sound of the song, which any of us could hear and see more clearly on YouTube. A feeling of connection to thousands of people gathered around the AMD stage makes this moment special. Each of us might have gone to see Robyn Hitchcock at the Austin Ventures stage or Thievery Corporation at the Barton Springs stage, but we chose this artist and this irretrievable moment on Friday, October 2, 2009 on some mashed down grass at Zilker Park in Austin, Texas.

The *ACL* Music Festival began as a very practical undertaking—in one sense, simply another chapter in the television show's ongoing quest to define and redefine itself in a changing musical world, and to find a stable funding source. As the twenty-fifth anniversary came and went, KLRU and *Austin City Limits* producers searched for options to sustain the program amid new economic conditions. Now divorced from the PBS funding system, sponsors underwrote the budget for the time being. Yet sponsorship followed a year-to-year commitment cycle often as uncertain as the shaky PBS budget cycles of the past.

For instance, longtime supporter Southwestern Bell dropped unceremoniously from the picture. Following the 1996 Telecommunications Act that lifted ownership restrictions on media, Southwestern Bell became SBC, bought AT&T, and reconfigured its way of doing business. The regional company had long sponsored community institutions like the annual Austin marathon and *Austin City Limits*. The newly consolidated AT&T realigned its overall marketing budget and made 25 percent cuts across the country. Local sponsorship for both the race and for *Austin City Limits* ended as a result. The latter once again scrambled to replace those funds. At one point around the turn of the century, the situation looked so bleak that KLRU took a loan to keep *Austin City Limits* going.[5]

The idea of a large-scale festival rose to the surface from several corners at once. Ed Bailey and others at KLRU looked at their ancillary pursuits, like the *Austin City Limits* DVD and CD releases, and pondered potential new revenue streams: "What can we do that's true to what we are? What other things could we create and put our name in association with it and have it be believable?"[6] KLRU's Board of Directors formed a Future of *ACL* Committee that included managers for local music acts and executives from prominent Austin-based companies like Dell. Their year-long "discovery" process included conversations about possible joint ventures with the House of Blues and Clear Channel, now LiveNation.[7]

The Future of *ACL* committee included Bill Stapleton, executive at Capital Sports & Entertainment (CSE). CSE had built its reputation as agent for the now-infamous biking champion Lance Armstrong, an Austin native and source of local pride before his spectacular fall from grace a decade later. The business expanded into music when they negotiated an advertising campaign with Johnson & Johnson for musician Shawn Colvin.[8] The Future of *ACL* conversations generated new visions. Around this time Stapleton and partner Bart Knaggs merged enterprises with promoter Charlie Jones, each hoping to expand on the foundation of Austin's musical reputation. They also hoped to contribute to the community whose quality of life and love of music they appreciated. Jones felt the time was ripe for a big outdoor music festival—something to fill the gap left after the demise of Aqua Fest, a summer event that, at its peak in 1987, drew 250,000 people to Town Lake but petered out over the next decade.[9]

Little by little the idea of an *Austin City Limits* Music Festival took on an aura of inevitability. People did research, traveling to music festivals to note what worked and what did not. The New Orleans Jazz & Heritage Festival stood out as the most direct inspiration. As Hickey explained, "We all went out there for research the first year we were launching *ACL* and had little notebooks and took notes." In the end, they "really wanted to mimic the New Orleans Jazz Festival.... Everyone thought the food was like a festival in itself because you could spend a whole day sampling. And so that was always our model."

Jones likewise recalled wanting the *ACL* Music Festival to mimic the way its New Orleans prototype communicates the culture and ambiance of its home city:

The television show and the Festival, to an outsider's perspective—yes, it's about music, but it's also about Austin. If you think of the New Orleans Jazz Fest, you don't necessarily think about just music and what's playing on the stage. You think about the culture of New Orleans, and the food, and Mardi Gras, and the street parades...you think of all the stuff that goes along with it when you think of New Orleans Jazz Fest. And when you think of *Austin City Limits*, you don't just necessarily think of the music that's being played on the stage. You think of the barbecue and you think of the live music scene in Austin. You think of the lakes and, you know, all that.

According to Jones, CSE "had reached the stage of 'how do we brand and name it? How does it develop trust?'" just when Mary Beth Rogers and others confronted the "branding and fundraising problems" at KLRU. For them the festival promised a fruitful business venture. For *Austin City Limits,* the festival augured potential freedom from the annual cycle of doubt and insecurity that came from reliance on either its parent television station, and thus PBS, or its commercial sponsors.

Jones reflected later that naming the festival for *Austin City Limits* "associated with the right brand, and the right group of people, in the right city, at the right time.... We had one chance right off the bat to deliver something that, over the past twenty-something years, had meant a lot to a lot of people." Across town the notion of an *ACL* Music Festival rang just as true. As Bailey put it, an Austin-based festival "would be believable in our own hometown—a festival that bears the *Austin City Limits* name, because we reflect Austin, and we're built from Austin. It's a natural extension of what we do, and it just needs to kind of mirror, or at least look like it belongs, to the heritage of what the show is."[10]

Both sides of this new venture contributed elements critical for its success. The *Austin City Limits* name carried enough political equity within the local community to convince the mayor, the city council, the Parks and Recreation department, and local neighborhoods to consider the notion of a major public event in its pristine Zilker Park. More generally, the reputation and credibility of *Austin City Limits,* all that its "brand" conveys, attracted the audience. CSE built on business savvy and skills like the ones Jones gained through his previous company, Middleman Productions.[11] They also enlisted well-connected booker and one-time competitor Charles Attal to bring in acts. Besides promotional expertise, CSE contributed the necessary capital resources for the risky and unpredictable task of putting on a major outdoor music event. While festivals remain one of the few business models in the topsy-turvy digital world of music that still portend large-scale potential profit, they also carry the potential to flop and flop hard.

Days before the event Stapleton worried that the company would lose its $1.25 million investment.[12] He fretted for naught. During that inaugural year, CSE recovered its investment and more. KLRU saw the fruits of its accumulated cultural capital, or the "intellectual property" *Austin City Limits* had built over decades. By then it was a "thirty-year-old trusted name that commands some respect and attention from people in the music industry."[13] KLRU and CSE entered into a five-year partnership, an experiment on the possibilities for public and private to each support and complement the aims of the other.

Attaching its name to the festival expanded the reach of *Austin City Limits*.[14] The festival helped *Austin City Limits* stretch toward younger audiences. As Jones said, "There is a very broad new audience that is paying attention to the television show on PBS or online or however they're getting their media and we had a lot to do with that, the Festival had a lot to do with it." By the same token, the *ACL* Music Festival attracts a more diverse audience in terms of income and age when compared with other major festivals. Its crowd generally includes older, more educated, and more well-off patrons than other major festivals: "In short, it is college-educated, good jobs, socially responsible, educated, cares about music, cares about the environment, appreciates a good time whether they live here or whether they are a tourist for a weekend."[15] Its link to the TV show shaped the appeal of the festival.

The *ACL* Music Festival presents more musical variety than similar events like Lollapalooza or Bonnaroo, a quality related to its Austin base and its connection to the historic eclecticism of *Austin City Limits*. In the lingo of the business, *ACL* is a "destination" festival, with its Austin locale very specifically part of its appeal.[16] As Lickona put it, "Coachella is out in the desert, Bonnaroo is in a cow pasture sixty miles outside of Nashville. The cool thing about *Austin City Limits* [Festival] is that it's in the central park, so to speak, of Austin right there in Zilker and it is easily accessible. People can walk there from home or from hotels or from wherever and they can hop in a cab or take a city bus to get there or to go home."[17] Furthermore, it takes place in a city park where people normally go with their families, making the event "much more accessible and family friendly."

If its Austin location fixes the festival to the city's reputation for musical vitality, the *Austin City Limits* name doubly anchors the event to the media institution, permeating it with cultural capital.[18] In that sense the identity of *Austin City Limits* and of the

Figure 8.4 The Austin Banjo Club performs on the sidewalk for the benefit of 2007 *ACL* Music Festival guests who wait to board the city buses that will transport them from downtown to Zilker.

festival that shares its name tangle up together. The festival demonstrates the shift of *Austin City Limits* from television program to a more diffuse indicator of good music in a tangible, on-the-ground way. In other words, the festival plays out in practice what it means for *Austin City Limits* to function as a "brand." Yet the relationship works in reverse as well. The show's loose musical parameters— which I boil down to some sort of balance between the liminal, the local, the centrist, and the groundbreaking—set the same loose terms for the festival. The event remains unconfined to any single genre. Thus it apparently fits with the history of the program and of its home city: "It seems like it's always been here. Because that's what it is branded on. *Austin City Limits* already had such…emotional trust…that the festival, even though it's only five years old, feels like it's been here forever."[19]

On the level of ideas, the partnership between KLRU and CSE made perfect sense. Their mutual aims and goals complemented one another in a yin-yang way. There were practical benefits as well. The station experienced relief from decades of budgetary night sweats. KLRU no longer sought sponsors for the show alone. CSE represented *Austin City Limits* in pursuing underwriters, in turn leveraging the established media brand to bring in more funding than the festival alone could do. During the five-year period they sold sponsorships as a package, giving underwriters already committed to the PBS broadcast, like Chevrolet and Anheuser-Busch, the first right of refusal.[20] This model fit changing corporate advertising strategies, which were moving beyond traditional media and integrating everything from soft drink-bottle labels to Twitter, or, in this case, from television shows to outdoor music celebrations.[21] Should underwriting fail to materialize, CSE agreed to backstop any budget holes for *Austin City Limits*.

Figure 8.5 The Del McCoury Band performs a bluegrass set during *ACL* 2007.

For the first time in its history KLRU could anticipate the funding for its most prominent program for five years out.[22] Furthermore, the joint arrangement positioned KLRU to complete the costly conversion to digital high definition (HD) technology, among other capital improvements. CSE meanwhile enjoyed a festival that grew from 77,000 attendees during its first year (between 35,000 and 42,000 on each of two days) to 155,000 the next when it expanded to three days; by its third year it topped out the park's capacity of 225,000 (75,000 each day).[23] Tickets have sold out faster and faster every year since. Hickey recalled in 2007, "We put 10,000 tickets up right after last year's festival and they crashed the system. We were not expecting it. They sold out in about 15 minutes."

Despite the benefits to both parties, wedding the goals, practices, and paradigms of a public television show with a popular and profitable music festival inevitably brought challenges as well. The two operations diverge in fundamental, paradigm-level ways. As *Austin City Limits* sound engineer David Hough explained it, the festival by its nature must be "new and adaptive" because dealing with that large a crowd requires it to be so. "We have our structure, which has been around so long everybody knows what they do, and they do it well" like a "well-oiled machine.... When the other structure at the fest started interfacing with this one, obviously there were some interfacing problems to work out."[24]

The two enterprises also differ dramatically in scale. The festival books over 130 acts every year, a number growing as of 2013 when the event expanded from one to two three-day weekends in October. By contrast the television show airs 13 hour-long episodes each year, which instills every individual booking with more weight. A single episode featuring, for instance, an artist from the Austin area significantly skews the percentage of local artists on a given season. Likewise a single international artist makes a stronger impression on the series as a whole than on the festival.

In the end, collaboration over day-to-day operations for both the festival and the television show proved to be invigorating, expansive, and, simultaneously, overly taxing for parties on both ends of the formal arrangement. Paradigms unavoidably bumped against one another. So, when the initial five years expired, both CSE and *Austin City Limits* people were ready to revisit their relationship.[25]

In 2007, Jones and Attal spun off a new company from CSE called C3 Presents specializing in major outdoor events like the *ACL* Festival. The two Charlies invited a third to the partnership, Charles Walker, who brought business acumen and experience with concert promotion from his prior position as LiveNation's North American president. The new company and KLRU refashioned their agreement. C3 wanted out of the television business. Instead its strategic focus shifted toward live events, including *ACL* Music Fest, and, eventually, a revitalized Lollapalooza in Chicago, both inaugurations for President Obama, concert bookings for Harrah's Casinos, the White House Easter Egg Roll, among others. C3 no longer wanted to bundle the *ACL* Music Festival with *Austin City Limits* on television; it wanted to bundle its festivals instead. The television people likewise looked to disentangle themselves from the festival business and focus on what they do best. Their renegotiated 10-year agreement sustains the mutually beneficial parts and drops the most troublesome parts. They still collaborate over bookings that interest both parties, but not as a contractual relationship. Instead the festival straight-out leases the *Austin City Limits* name and logo from KLRU in exchange for a percentage of gate receipts, guaranteeing a base fee that covers the show's production costs.

Philanthropic funds from the festival benefit the nonprofit arm of the local parks administration, a relationship partly necessitated by the impact of the event on Zilker Park. C3 funded a $2.5 million renovation of the park in 2008. Too much foot traffic and not enough time for soil compaction destroyed some of this work during the next year's festival, but repairs followed in short order. Apart from its festival home, the infusion of capital funds paid for bike trail improvements and other updates in parks all over Austin. When all is said and done, C3's local base of operations, and subsequent investment of many of its people within the local community, further distinguishes the Austin event from other major festivals.

The festival created the capacity to bring major music acts to the city of Austin for the first time. In this way the *ACL* Festival repositioned Austin in relation to the music world, and, by extension, repositioned *Austin City Limits*. As Bailey put it, the festival "creatively gave us a lot more crayons in our box" because "this show has always relied on geographic opportunity."[26] In other words, the nonprofit enterprise, *Austin City Limits*, more often than not books bands who come to the area for other reasons. Artists find it easier to do a taping for union scale when they also have a higher-paying gig nearby. Austin long lacked a big site for music. "We couldn't book a band because they go to San Antonio, Dallas, or Houston, [where] they have big venues that take their tours.... If they can sell 36,000 seats, they want to sell 36,000 seats because that's what pays for the entourage of the ten semi trucks of the Dixie Chicks ... or the Rolling Stones, or whoever."[27]

That changed after the festival in what several crew members refer to as the "Coldplay effect," for the first stadium-size act to appear on *Austin City Limits*.[28] ACL created the practical conditions necessary to "tackle new talent opportunities."[29] In so doing, the festival adjusted the scale on which *Austin City Limits* could carry on—a matter of expansion rather than rupture. Now concentrated tapings flank the weekend of the ACL Music Festival because a number of bands drawn to the outdoor event stay in town long enough to tape an episode. During the September 2006 ACL Music Festival, Van Morrison, the New Orleans Social Club, The Raconteurs, Los Lonely Boys, Cat Power, Calexico, and KT Tunstall stayed in town to tape a show around the festival weekend. Damian Marley, the first reggae act on *Austin City Limits*, also played both festival and show.

Shows like the one by Marley indicate ways in which the festival producers pushed their public television partners to broaden the scope of the programming and, therefore, broaden the viewing audience. The festival prodded along the spirit of eclecticism and experimentation that has been part of the *Austin City Limits* story all along. Given its scale, a large breadth of bookings makes sound business sense. In Jones's words, "You can't have 125 bands in the same demographic, or the same genre of music.... I think our median age is 34. In order to hit at the median age of 34 you can't just have new and upcoming rock bands.... You've got to have across the board."[30]

The last year when the synergy between the *ACL* Music Festival and the *Austin City Limits* television show was formal and overt everywhere I looked was 2006. That year the marquee simply read "*Austin City Limits* Music Festival."[31] The festival joined visual imagery to the musical experience, deliberately connecting the musical past with the present. Throughout the grounds, festival attendees encountered giant enlargements of historical images from some of the classic episodes like Stevie Ray Vaughan and Johnny Cash. A shade tent sponsored by Blackstone Winery featured "The *Austin City Limits* Experience." I recall plopping myself with gratitude into one of the plastic Adirondack chairs. From there I reveled in the sight of a big television screen showing clips of *Austin City Limits*, while also taking in the drift from two live stages at once, Okkervil River playing on one and Wolf Parade on another.[32]

At that moment it was obvious that the meaning of this event, like the broader meaning of *Austin City Limits*, springs from live and mediated sources at once. The moment existed within a symbolic economy where the present intersected the past, and where the so-called real world intersected the world of ideas.[33] People buy tickets to this festival before they ever know who is playing. That indicates the extent to which the overall experience defines the event more than the specific musical lineup. As Hickey summed it up, "People come for the experience. They don't want to miss it. We deliver that good experience."

Any festival includes the sense of "being there" as part of its attraction.[34] Several people I met at the *ACL* Music Festival over the years traveled regularly and extensively to similar events. The willingness to fork over money, time, and effort in getting there establishes common ground among individuals present at the gathering. Attending a major festival takes on aspects of a secular pilgrimage.[35] By concentrating a variety of performers in close succession, along with the close company of like-minded music lovers, festivals create a unique musical circumstance. There are cheaper, more comfortable, and more focused ways to enjoy musical sounds in and of themselves, but something beyond the music itself moves festival audiences to gather. This is not new.

South Texas boasts a long tradition of outdoor musical events that presage *ACL*. Most prominent among them are Willie Nelson's

Figure 8.6 A crowd shot looking toward the stage where Common performs during *ACL* 2007.

Fourth of July picnics, which inspired magazine and other writers to capture the mystique of "being there" in words. Despite the financial failure of the three-day Dripping Springs Reunion in 1972, *Texas Observer* journalist Dean Rindy nevertheless noted the "subtle delight that comes upon people when they are free in fine weather and full of sunshine and booze…a sort of communal high."[36] Early press release writers for *Austin City Limits* tapped into this mystique, drawing connections between Nelson's picnics and the new PBS show. They included the firsthand "impressions of one intrepid, mud-covered picnic-goer": "For all the physical misery of baking under a high and hot Texas sun, you come away glad you went. It's an event—people want to be able to say, 'I was there!'"[37]

Nelson's picnics belong to an era of big music festival "happenings," firmly fixed in the late 1960s and early 1970s. Someone put up the capital funds for the space, equipment, and performers, then hoped for the best. Profit came from ticket sales. Although "being there" remains the force drawing participants to spend considerable money, time, and energy to attend, *ACL* belongs to a new era. Festivals these days anticipate profits as much from sponsorships as from ticket sales. They sell sponsors the chance to reach "engaged" audiences.[38] They deliver sponsors effective marketing and, by the same token, deliver audiences lower ticket prices than otherwise possible. They keep an entrepreneurial eye past the three-day weekend, toward the event's long-term sustainability. In short, contemporary major festival organizers bring a level of business savvy and sophistication absent from their predecessors in previous decades.

Festival sponsorship extends beyond simply finding businesses willing to spend money to have their name on a festival stage. Sponsorship becomes part of a symbolic economy where the indescribable meanings and emotions associated with one brand can resonate with the identity of the festival or create tension with it. So sponsorship offers from Axe Deodorant or McDonald's might very well be turned away. On the other hand, sponsorship from Xbox makes sense because gaming and music go hand in hand: Walmart, no; Sears, no; Target, yes.[39] Sponsorships from staple Austin businesses like H.E.B., Austin Ventures, and Advanced Micro Devices, a California-based company with an office in Austin, make sense because locale is essential to the *ACL* Music Festival's identity. Modern events like *ACL* Music Festival work well when they situate material experience within a conceptual frame that resonates happily. These relationships, always shifting, between symbolic and corporeal reality, shape the meaning for the whole event. Music plays a critical role in that, as do value-laden goals like eco-friendliness or carbon neutrality.[40]

A laid-back vibe and easygoing behavior distinguishes audiences at the *ACL* Music Festival from those at other major festivals. Statistically speaking, *ACL* boasts remarkably few arrests for the number of people gathered there.[41] Reasons for this run deeper than its more mature demographic. The atmosphere stems once more from the entire symbolic economy that makes up the *ACL* Music Festival. As Jones expressed it, the audience atmosphere is "not just about how many security officers you have."

It goes all the way back to the band booking, to our marketing, our messaging, the information we give our patrons prior to them getting in the door. The band booking does have something to do with it. The location has something to do with it. But there are just a lot of factors that come into play that put together a large group of people that simultaneously have a very good time and behave.[42]

As much as anything, media shape the meaning of the *ACL* Music Festival by giving it life that extends before, during, and after the on-the-ground event in Zilker Park each fall. Web-media specialists nurture that life, for example by posting artist profiles in the weeks or months leading up to the festival. Profiles generate interest in the bands before the event, creating excitement and anticipation, even building a sense of community among audience members. Some of these audience members blog about the musicians or the event itself, and the best examples get pulled in, expanding the web of communications about *ACL*.

The technology that facilitates this flow changes all the time. As Hickey told me, "I don't even think there was an iPod when we launched the festival." They concentrated on building an email list during the first couple of years. Then came MySpace. Facebook at first started only for college students and then expanded for everyone. Hickey said, "93 percent of people come to *ACL* because they heard about it from a friend, not because they saw it in a newspaper advertisement or saw it on television. Friends told them about it." Within the constant ebb and flow of information circulating across multiple forms of media, an event like the *ACL* Music Festival must stand out enough to function as a strange attractor competing with other strange attractors. The situation demands constant vigilance:

> It seems like every week we're adding 2,500 new friends on Facebook. And, you know, and to that point, those friends have their networks, and when they're saying that they are going to attend *ACL* or they like a band that's playing on the *ACL* Festival or they're going to share their schedule that they've made, it hits so many more people. It's pretty cool in just trying to figure out how it all works.[43]

During the festival itself people experience the event in a way not imaginable at Dripping Springs back in 1972. They experience it as both live and mediated at the same time. At the entry gate, festival goers are handed a free download code for an extensive playlist of festival acts so that they can listen privately to artists they saw publicly long after the festival ends. Scanning the top of the crowds standing before any *ACL* tent (or most any other performance, really), a sea of cell phones waves overhead in an attempt to capture this fleeting moment. In fact, its transitory nature perhaps intensifies the role of media in shaping the meaning of the *ACL* Music Festival. As sociologist Sarah Thornton suggests in a different musical context, "Media confirm, spread and consolidate cultural perceptions—even amongst those who were there to experience the event. Their predictions have repeated if unpredictable effects."[44] Unlike the television show, which can be recorded from the broadcast, watched in a rerun, or in some cases purchased on DVD, the Festival is over when it's over. Afterward, the virtual community posts its videos, discusses its favorite moments, debates whether or not this year surpassed last year's lineup, and anticipates the day and time tickets for next year become available.

Live and mediated worlds intersect at any major festival.[45] They do so uniquely at the *ACL* Music Festival. It was obvious under the shade tent when I sat taking in two live performers and two TV episodes all at once. More often the connections happen in subtler ways. These intersections between live and mediated worlds potentially deepen the experience for an *ACL* participant, who might find himself on a field watching Van Morrison in the distance, or maybe Lucinda Williams, or Willie Nelson, and connect that moment to the musical vitality of the city, or to the spirit of eclecticism that links at least back to the progressive country days. He might later catch an episode of *Austin City Limits* on television

Figure 8.7 Skies were clear during *ACL* 2006, leaving an open line of vision from Zilker Park toward the *real* Austin skyline.

and find himself transported back to that same grassy patch (or dusty patch or muddy patch, depending on the year), with the music bouncing all around, the moon rising full, the Austin skyline stretching out in the distance, chicken cone in hand. Since the festival began, *Austin City Limits* occupies several spaces or places at once. They are geographic, mediated, and conceptual: at Austin's Zilker Park during a three-day weekend (now two weekends) in the early fall; on the PBS television lineup for 13 hour-long episodes each year; and as an idea, or a brand, with the potential to motivate, excite, attract, or move people to check out some music. A new facet of meaning opened up with a new *Austin City Limits* venue and studio in February 2011.

[9]

AUSTIN CITY LIMITS
EQUALS BIG WAVE

When after 37 seasons *Austin City Limits* moved from Studio 6A at station KLRU to the brand-new *ACL* Live at the Moody Theater venue, its crew brought only a few things with them. The camera pedestals made the trek, fitted with new cameras and new lenses, because they allow the operators to dolly up, truck left, and perform all the other moves that mold the look of the show. They also brought the old artificial tree branch that hung high along the bleachers in 6A. Sentiment motivated that more than anything, but the tree branch also defined the foreground for a signature wide-and-from-behind-the-audience shot that often opened and closed an *Austin City Limits* episode. The big camera crane responsible for those shots retired from service. Longtime floor manager Ray Lucero got nostalgic about it, just for a moment: "I don't know what's going to become of it. It's got a lot of our soul with it."[1] The dressing room photos of past performers came too and still hang behind the artists during the end-of-show interviews.

They planned on moving the stage, but as producer Jeff Peterson explained, they wound up reconstructing a similar one instead. Smaller than the industry standard, the stage has played an essential role in realizing the show's vision since the start.[2] Peterson should know; he has been around *Austin City Limits* since he began as an audio engineer at KLRU in 1978. Peterson eventually was hired to work closely on *Austin City Limits*, evolving over the years to his current producer post. From his point of view the smaller stage size is essential. Besides determining many of the camera angles, the stage brings band members in close to one another and to the audience. A large stadium group like the Dave Matthews Band, accustomed to playing spread out, performs relatively shoulder to shoulder on *Austin City Limits*. Cameras can capture shots with more than one band member in action at a time, but, more importantly, their proximity intensifies the energy that passes among musicians during the act of making music. Just as critically the low height amplifies communication between performers and the live audience. As Terry Lickona put it, "You can see every face in the room. The low stage makes it easier to connect with the audience."[3]

The studio audience has been a critical part of *Austin City Limits* from the beginning. Leonard Cohen, whose 1989 broadcast was also his first US television appearance, famously paused mid-set to ask, "Is this a real audience—or have you all been brought in from occupational therapy or something?"[4] The show's first producer, Paul Bosner, saw the relationship between performance and audience as "magic." In an early memo, he wrote, "Difficult though it may be, the essence that is to be recorded on tape is that magic that floats back and forth between the musician and the audience, a magic that permeates the atmosphere."[5]

An early document promoting *Austin City Limits* to station programmers refers to the show's "magic" as well, but expresses its founding vision in more concrete terms of how space design and camera work emphasize the energy and the relationship between performers and audience members:

> The set is structured to re-create the club experience as much as possible, and in some respects, the single, shared environment created is even more intimate than the clubs themselves, providing continuous and direct visual relationships between audience and musician as well as among musicians. In addition, the camera work attempts to capture the electricity of the live studio performance by sensing the subtle energy exchanges between musician and audience. In this way, *Austin City Limits* brings new textures and dimensions to music for television, but the real magic is in the music and the music is alive and growing in the heart of Texas, Austin.[6]

Bosner wanted every shot to include audience in the background. To that end he arranged the performance area so that people sat on carpet out in front of the performer and on small risers to the sides and around back. As David Hough recalled, Bosner "had this concept that there was this three-way feedback loop going on. The band would play, and the audience would react to that, and the band would react to that, and so this thing would build up as the night goes on, and as the beer flowed."[7] Later directors moved the audience from behind the stage, placing more focus on the artists and gaining more control over what the cameras pick up.

Two conditions helped prime the live audience at *Austin City Limits*. One was scarcity. Tickets cost nothing but historically took great effort to obtain. Holding a ticket did not even guarantee entry, only the opportunity to line up in high hopes. That circumstance lent a special kind of energy to the gathering. Beer helped too. Lone Star, an early *Austin City Limits* underwriter, established a precedent for free beer that helped ensure a loose, interactive studio crowd. With the exception of the one season when UT President Lorene Rogers tried to impose a no-beer-in-the-building rule—sparking a mild community uproar—free beer continued despite the switch sometime before the show's tenth anniversary from Lone Star to Budweiser and later to Ziegenbock.[8]

The unpredictability of live performance added potential excitement for both performers and audiences, sometimes before the music began. Studio 6A audiences witnessed their share of idiosyncratic moments over the years, which populate the annals of *Austin City Limits* history. Ray Charles once had a bat flying around his dressing room, inspiring a moment's panic for one of his roadies. Ray Lucero grabbed the butterfly net he kept on hand, removed the critter, and the show went on.[9] Country-folk-rocker pianist Tracy Nelson came on stage to perform and set a bottle of whiskey on top of the instrument as if the studio were a saloon.[10] During Doug Sahm's taping in Season 1, a young woman in a "granny dress" danced her way to the front row then, "all of a sudden, she reached down and pulled the hem of her dress up over her head, and she wasn't wearing anything underneath."[11]

Other distinctly live moments include the taping Texas guitar legend Joe Ely did near Halloween in 1984 (Season 10, 1985), when half the audience came in costumes. Ely invited the audience to join him on stage, a moment he later recalled to a reporter. "'I remember seeing the camera crew making motions like, 'No, no, you can't do this!' . . . It was like a wild dream, with an audience full of ghouls and goblins.'"[12] The resulting crush blocked Ely from reaching the microphone during the song "Fingernails." Ricky Van Shelton began to play solo when his keyboard player failed to return to the stage for the encore (Season 13, 1988 or Season 16, 1991). When the keyboard part suddenly fell in, he turned to see an audience member who had taken the stage and was play-ing along flawlessly. Most legendary is the entire taping of Kinky Friedman that finally became available on DVD only 32 years after the fact.[13] Friedman's performance was so over-the-top with pro-vocative songs like "They Ain't Making Jews Like Jesus Anymore" and the send-up of Merle Haggard's "Okie from Muskogee" titled "Arsehole from El Paso" that PBS forbade its airing.

Crowds once jammed cheek-by-jowl into Studio 6A, often 500 or as many as 800 strong. The most apocryphal incident from Austin City Limits lore happened when a power outage inter-rupted Kris Kristofferson's taping in Season 7 (1982). The story plays out in various ways: it was a lightning storm, or a rat in the electrical system, or a rat in the electrical system during a light-ning storm. Regardless of its source, sudden pitch black descended on the packed audience. . . . The crowd sat peacefully sipping beer in the total darkness, holding up cigarette lighters and singing "London Homesick Blues" until Austin City Limits volunteers with flashlights led them calmly down six flights of stairs and out the building. Someone must have led Kristofferson to safety as well, though his predicament seems to fall outside the crux of the tale. The occurrence moved the local fire marshal to impose a limit on future Austin City Limits audiences, first to 450 people, and later reduced further to 300.[14]

The number of bodies present affects a sound recording. Hough told me before the relocation to the Moody:

> I remember back before we were discovered when we had B.B. King in Season 8 in this room and we had over 800 peo-ple in the audience standing in the aisles and I remember the audio: recording that sound of that big a crowd. And I think I even saved some of that audience reaction on tape just to have

it 'cause it was a big, big sound. And then when the fire marshal started knocking our size down to 400 and then 300…and
then if we have a band when people start to leave early, I can
hear how the room changes tone and becomes more cavernous
and hollow, and the early days I never heard that.[15]

The size of the new Moody Theater solves the long-standing
challenge of audience numbers in Studio 6A, with 1,800 seats
when open to full capacity. The original vision was to install a cur-
tain that would obscure the third, highest level for smaller shows.[16]
However, the venue has been so successful, including expansion
of the station's "Friends of KLRU" program, that the curtaining
never materialized. The larger audience, thus, increases the energy
in the room. As Lickona reflected,

> I could feel the difference right away after all those years back
> in Studio 6A, coming out on stage to introduce the shows each
> night when we had about 300–350 people in the room. And
> from the very first taping here when I would come out on stage
> and the roar of the crowd—it was palpably bigger, louder—and
> I could just sense the fact that there were that many more peo-
> ple in the room.[17]

The *ACL* Live venue solves another issue related to capacity.
With greater reliance on sponsors over the years, the ratio of raw
enthusiasm to intellectual curiosity could sometimes dampen
energy in the room. A ticket to the show was about the only physical perk *Austin City Limits* could offer sponsors and donors, and
they sometimes held as many as half the tickets aside. These seats
did not always fill with the kind of enthusiastic fan who sings along
with the lyrics to every tune or communicates bodily back to the

performer. The new space makes room for all kinds of concertgoers. It accommodates a crowd big enough to generate energy, and arranges it so that the less intense audience likely migrates to the mezzanine and more demonstrative fans populate the floor area or bleachers, in closest proximity to the artist and to the cameras.

The space created some new circumstances when it came to the audience's role in taping a broadcast. Nothing substitutes for trial and error when learning your way through an unfamiliar situation. It was not the best idea, for example, to tape a Widespread Panic showcase performance during SXSW that also happened to fall on St. Patrick's Day. Widespread Panic had done two other shows in the past, but there were 300–350 people in the room then as opposed to 2,000. On top of that, between the reputation of Widespread Panic fans for their "excess and enthusiasm" and the legacy of revelry Ireland's patron left behind, most of the audience came to the show already blitzed.[18] Two and a half hours later the crew was dead on their feet and everyone agreed it had been too much.

Adjusting to new rhythms in a new space took practice, particularly since *ACL Live* at the Moody serves a dual purpose. In other words, the space demands more preparation work for each taping. Back at Studio 6A, staff members stepped comfortably into their assigned places on a taping day. It was almost as easy as walking in, flipping on the lights, and being "ready to go except for setting up for the band."[19] These days, taping *Austin City Limits* feels like doing a remote every time. That adjustment has been the biggest.

For one thing, the venue uses a higher stage, which means it must be rolled away for tapings and the smaller *Austin City Limits* stage rolled in its place. Likewise the bleachers need to be rolled out and assembled for tapings. They presented unanticipated obstacles during construction and setup once they arrived via cargo boat from a Belgium company, the only one willing to build them to specifications. Arriving in 8,000-pound sections, the bleachers first proved too bulky for the freight elevator, then so precise that slightly unlevel places in the floor prevented locking them into place. A team of Belgian engineers flew to Austin for the installation, but not before at least one early show happened with only half the bleachers in place.[20] From the staff point of view, finally settling the bleachers helped the room begin to feel familiar.[21]

Even six months after the space opened, technical glitches remained. The new skyline, for instance, bigger and more prominent with the dome and the tower backlit, would suddenly begin blinking in the middle of a taping and no one could figure out why. Other hiccups happened with the fancy new software-driven video equipment for grabbing the wide shots once covered by the old Wizard-of-Oz crane. The Italian-designed system uses a robotic camera mounted on a track to travel the wall just below the first balcony, but its smooth functioning took some time to achieve.

The new challenges at the Moody hover front and center for Lucero, *Austin City Limits* floor manager since 1980, whose experience dates back to the beginnings when he worked on KRLN's bilingual children's show, *Carrascolendas*. Someone asked him to pull cable for a new program they were trying out, which turned out to be the pilot episode for *Austin City Limits*.[22] He worked lighting, then the crane camera, until finally moving into his current role. In contrast to 6A, they often start with a bare stage now. "We have to bring in lights. We have to bring in the staging, plants, all that—cameras, everything.... In the old place, all the cameras are already set up. All we have to do is roll them into the studio and, you know, everything else was kind of set."[23] Likewise, after taping, everything gets cleared: the cameras, the plants all move to storage, and the cityscape gets curtained off. Oftentimes the stage itself gets cleared away and the higher venue stage restored to its place.

Some cherished rituals and traditions stayed behind at Studio 6A. Both the backstage setup and all the work involved in breakdown after each taping precluded the usual after-show get-together. For years staff had gathered after each show, usually late at night, for a beer, a dish or two prepared by longtime KLRU Chief Engineer David Kuipers, and a first view of the night's work.[24] The "signing wall," too, remains back on the second floor of KLRU. For decades crew members and artists left their marks on the wall, now memorialized in *Austin City Limits: 35 Years in Photographs*, a book of Scott Newton's photography with commentary by Terry Lickona. The book includes Lickona standing before the wall, behind him a sketch of ocean waves drawn there by Pearl Jam's Eddie Vedder, along with his caption, "Austin City Limits Equals Big Wave."[25]

Other moments linger only in memory. Nearly every *Austin City Limits* performer brings to mind an anecdote for at least one member of the crew. Some of these are transcendent moments available to them only because of the up-close circumstances of their work. Associate producer Leslie Nichols recalled watching Dolly Parton rehearse. She and then associate producer Susan Caldwell pulled their chairs near the stage to watch. Parton sang "Mountain Angel" six feet away, looking right at them, while Nichols and Caldwell sat crying their eyes out for the duration of the song. Afterward Parton smiled. "That was plumb pitiful, wasn't it?" she said.[26]

Another favorite revolves around Lyle Lovett, who recorded at least 12 times over the years. Before performing there, Lovett had attended *Austin City Limits* as a guest in the audience more than once. The first time he taped a show, the editing crew inserted an old audience shot so that the final episode cuts from Lovett performing to Lovett clapping from the bleachers.[27] Lyle Lovett maintained a special connection to *Austin City Limits*. When it came time for the final taping in Studio 6A, he performed there one last time. At the end people cried and joined him on stage to sing a final number. Lucero recalled, "We all got up on stage—camera operators, Terry Lickona, myself, Gary…and we harmonized to "Closing Time."[28]

Despite changes, *Austin City Limits* staffers have little time for nostalgia, and their core task remains intact: to achieve "a natural environment" so that the artists "come in and get up on the stage and do their show like they would anywhere else and not feel the pressures of doing television so much."[29] Likewise they want the audience to be able to "just focus on the music and not feel like they're being subjected to a television production that makes them uncomfortable. So we have to work even harder to achieve that net result at the end of the day." Ultimately, it is hard not to appreciate seeing and hearing live music in the Moody. As Lickona put it, "most people enjoy the experience of coming…because it's still the best place in Austin to see and hear live music.… So even if it's not quite as cozy as the original studio, I think people still dig it."

Indeed, when the time came for The Decemberists to tape their second episode for Season 37, now in the Moody, it is easy to forget anything has changed. Lickona takes the stage to introduce the band and thank the sponsors. He stands farther away and looks a little smaller here, but his big radio voice carries well. Once the show begins there's camera operator Vance Holmes mouthing the lyrics along with lead singer Colin Meloy. (I assume Holmes isn't really singing—Gary Menotti surely wouldn't appreciate a headset serenade.) The Decemberists' performance peaked during "The Rake's Song," with its repeated chant "All right, all right, all

Figure 9.1 Gillian Welch appears on the control booth monitors in the back of the house at the new *ACL* Live at the Moody Theater during a double taping in August 2011. She followed The Decemberists.

right" over syncopated drum accents. At the climactic moment, not only drummer John Moen, but Jenny Conlee, Sara Watkins, and Chris Funk all doubled the rhythmic accents on the floor toms. It was one of those highly theatrical moments that makes The Decemberists so much fun to see in person.

From any seat in the house, the acoustics inside *ACL* Live at the Moody are impressive. Music steered its design from the earliest planning stages. Nashville-based engineer Steven Durr devised the acoustics and the sound systems. Behind the scenes, the production and control rooms, the back of house, the dressing rooms all follow specifications of the *Austin City Limits* team who brought their years of expertise to the project.[30] Out front Durr wanted to replicate some of the beloved, if accidental,

Figure 9.2 The audience out front takes in Gillian Welch and David Rawlings along with the new skyline backdrop.

characteristics of Studio 6A. It was, after all, a television studio commandeered for music.

Durr aimed to take the long-standing *Austin City Limits* team and, in his words, "move them into a new space and maintain the same warm and real sound they are famous for and loved [*sic*].[31] Maintaining a sense of intimacy in spite of the larger size was key. For Durr that close quality invigorates the live audience which, in turn, determines the success of any televised show, regardless of broadcast audio quality. As he put it, "I'm in the emotions business…. Amplified sound is simply the transfer medium and the way we convey the emotions of music."[32]

Thanks to eight feet of concrete above and below, vibrations and noise from the street stay out of the concert space. Music and crowd noise stay in. The building entrance and exit is located at the end of high, high stairs, through 400-pound doors. Lickona joked once that "between those doors and the stairs, I could quit my gym membership and I'd be in just as good a shape exercising here every time I come to work." The layers of concrete keep tapings and events in *ACL* Live from disturbing guests and condominium residents at the 37-floor W Hotel complex that rises alongside it.

The care and deliberation that went into soundproofing the new *ACL* Live venue manifests contemporary developments in Austin, where its civic leaders regularly channel collective energy into prodding forward the ongoing municipal conversation about music. For one example, in answer to a general sense of local crisis about the oversupply of musicians struggling to make a living, a 15-member Live Music Task Force (LMTF) formed to confront the issues. Its members worked for most of 2008 on recommendations for sweetening and sustaining the attraction of Austin for local musicians. After all, noteworthy as SXSW and the *ACL* Music Festival are, they do not provide constant employment and financial stability to keep Austin musicians at home. Likewise the audiences for these events are geared up for intense, expensive, and exhausting live musical experiences; that differs from an audience who regularly supports local live venues on a weekend-by-weekend basis.

The LMTF recommendations, developed via four subcommittees—Venues, Entertainment Districts, Musician Services, and Sound Enforcement & Control—were voted on and approved by the City Council in January of the following year. Their final document summons a spirit of coalition-building between city officials, musicians, venue owners, and neighborhoods, all of whom have a stake in Austin's "Live Music Capital" status and, therefore, in the benefits (economic) and challenges (noise pollution) that reputation brings.

They recommended consolidating oversight for Live Music Venues (LMVs) rather than its piecemeal dispersal between police, watershed, and parking departments. They advised closer communications between city government and groups that advocate for and support working musicians, such as the Health Alliance for Austin Musicians (HAAM) and the Austin Music Foundation. They counseled the need for more resources like health care access and affordable housing to attract and sustain working musicians. They took on practical concerns, including permitting, parking, load-in spaces, and transportation, each important to uphold existing entertainment districts and develop new ones. And they addressed noise control and requirements for soundproofing in new building construction.

I first saw the building project when it was under construction, at least six months from opening. We zipped up fluorescent green vests and donned specially made hard hats stamped with logos for *Austin City Limits*, W Hotel, Stratus Properties, and other partners in the project. The bare slabs and stud walls outlined places that our guide, Freddy Fletcher, already saw clearly in his mind. Fletcher had worked for at least five years on the project up until this time. This muddy area will become the valet drop-off point and drive-through hotel entrance. Here is the back of the house, where green rooms, the audiovisual studios (wired to every other part of the venue), and office spaces stand. The freight elevator could fit an SUV, and a smaller high-speed elevator lets the artists move from their hotel rooms to the stage without running into the public. The front of the house includes bars and bathrooms on every floor and, on the second floor, a photo gallery to display classic *Austin City Limits* shots by photographer Scott Newton.

Industrial fans blow across the space where the hotel entrance and lobby will be. It will have a full kitchen and 11 different bars, including one that can be closed off for private gatherings. And this is where the living room goes—all W hotels have a living room. "I plan to put a Steinway in here for mom," says Freddy Fletcher, "so she can come in and play it when she's not out on the road." Fletcher's mom is Bobbie, Willie Nelson's sister and long time piano player in Willie's band. In fact she played with him some 40 years ago when Nelson taped the pilot for *Austin City Limits.*

I imagine a much younger Fletcher, perhaps in the audience or backstage for that occasion, with no clue as to where this moment would lead. Now he represents Nelson in business interests that include two recording studios, a boutique record label (Pedernales), and as a partner in the multi-use development. In the design-planning phase Fletcher traveled along with Stratus Properties executives to other venues and sat down with their operators to talk about what works and what does not. Fletcher wants this venue to be there for his grandchildren.[33]

A little more than a year after the construction tour, I traveled back to see the end result. Now completed, the W Hotel itself is the kind of place where the desk staff greets guests by name as they come and go, and the "Good Afternoon" floor mats in front of the elevator change to "Good Evening" floor mats. Scott Newton's photographs hang in every room of the W Austin hotel as well, available for purchase. Kinky Friedman was on the wall in my room. The swimming pool is gorgeous, long and skinny, with a small water spill running its length, flanked by lounge chairs and big beach umbrellas.

At least around cocktail hour no one swims, despite the Austin August temperature that tops 105°F. Rather, the scene looks as if the camera crew from *The Bachelorette* might emerge at any moment to catch these beautiful people, beautifully posed, each with a drink dangling from one hand. Where do they all come

Figure 9.3 The poolside at the W Hotel is quiet during an early August morning in 2011.

from? Three late-20-something men stand thigh-high in the water and pass small talk about shaving their pecs. "I don't mind chest hair, but I don't want to be like some bear." "All the Mexican resorts have saline pools like this one now.... It's much more gentle on the skin than chlorine."[34] The beer-stained rug on the floor of the Armadillo seems pretty far away. Back then Willie Nelson gave that whole scene a coherence people could wrap their minds (and ears) around, including people who started *Austin City Limits* in response. Looking out toward Nelson's eight-foot-high bronze likeness now standing before the Moody, he still offers a satisfying sense of continuity to all that has transpired since.

Had things gone precisely as Terry Lickona envisioned, the first taping in the new *ACL* Live venue would have been Willie Nelson and Family. What more fitting tribute could there be for the musician whose life and music signify the story of *Austin City Limits* and of Austin itself over the past four decades? How could things come more full circle, simultaneously closing one era and beginning another? Instead, plans unfolded in the compromise-laden way of any long-term, successfully established enterprise. The Gala Committee for KLRU, wanting to maximize the opening for their annual fundraising efforts, set a firm date for the event six months in advance, February 24. Nelson was unavailable that weekend, and the stars failed to line up. Saturn was nowhere in sight. In the end, Willie Nelson gave the first performance in the Moody Theater on February 13, 2011, not taped for broadcast. The Steve Miller Band performed the Gala, as well as the first episode in the Moody.

Apart from the opening act, booking the first full season in the Moody (Season 37, 2011–2012) brought many of the same joys and challenges as any other. Lickona has a "hit list" of people he has been pursuing for 25 years or so. That year he finally got Randy Newman to do a taping. Stevie Wonder and Paul Simon didn't pan out, but there's always next year.[35] The biggest disappointment came when Adele had to cancel due to a bad case of laryngitis. Throat-related health problems caused her to call off her entire American tour, which included an *Austin City Limits* taping. In the meantime her career exploded and, when they re-booked her American schedule, including stops in Texas, her management had decided that any full-length American television program would compete with their plans to record a live concert at Royal Albert Hall for DVD release. She would have been the season opener. Radiohead kicked things off instead.

Perhaps all that is apropos, since nothing about the *Austin City Limits* story is predictable or neat or square. Its long and varied history operates at once as a core challenge and an asset. The challenge comes from the fact that so long a history presents end-less potential to alienate somebody somewhere. A viewer's expectations for *Austin City Limits* can solidify according to the timing and circumstances of that individual's most memorable encounter with it. Audiences include, in no particular order, local Austin community members, critics, PBS powers-that-be, local musicians, national and international musicians, corporate sponsors, the board of trustees, the older television audience, the younger television audience, the festival collaborators, the venue owners, the Gala committee, and so on.

Each audience brings a different agenda and set of priorities. Some long-standing board members, for example, lobby for George Strait or Roseanne Cash to come on again. Sponsors like AMD or Anheuser-Busch or Heineken want to participate in something that's "plugged in," hip, or cool so they may press for artists with a contemporary buzz. Other sponsors push specifically for programming aimed at a clear group, for example, Latino viewers, because that company hopes to expand its market within that population group.

As Ed Bailey told me in 2006, there are "people who think that all we should be doing is bluegrass, guitarists, Stevie Rays, the Lyles of the world. It got in their head that that's what we are, and they're not embracing the fact that we're bringing on Spoon, and that's still Austin. Spoon is Austin…today. What Made Milwaukee Famous is Austin today."[36] What epitomizes the show can depend on when a viewer first fell in love with *Austin City Limits*. Bailey recalled a letter he received during Season 30 (2004–2005), complaining about what seemed to its writer a particular programming travesty. It read something like "Bright Eyes can't sing, who is this guy? You guys are nuts! Bring back Jerry Jeff Walker!"[37]

The wheedling and shoving, collision and fusion of competing priorities accounts for how *Austin City Limits* stays a relevant and vital musical force so many years down the road. It is an expansion, not rupture, of meaning. Bailey gave me an example of how different priorities among competing voices offset one another and ultimately create the breadth of music that distinguishes *Austin City Limits*. Season 32 (2006–2007) included Juanes and Ladysmith Black Mambazo, both international but quite different musical acts. No single set of criteria or group of voices led to their bookings, nor any others that year. Both helped balance a season that also featured the Dixie Chicks and James Blunt, Van Morrison and the New Orleans Social Club, Corinne Bailey Rae and The Raconteurs, along with Sufjan Stevens, James McMurtry, the Gourds, and Alejandro Escovedo, the latter three based in Austin.

Juanes is a Grammy-winning, top-selling artist in the Latin musical world, and "a U2-sized star in Colombia."[38] To book him for *Austin City Limits* might draw a wider television audience than normal and introduce audiences previously unaware of Juanes to his music. A group like Ladysmith Black Mambazo might lead to a similar result but for different reasons. Less commercially hot, Ladysmith enjoys an international reputation as now-classic ambassadors for South African *mbube*, some 20 years after their famous collaboration with Paul Simon. When the possibility of booking them for *Austin City Limits* came onto the radar, the mission of public television came to the fore of the decision-making process. As Bailey mused on it, "We've never done anything like that.... I mean that's a gift.... You don't put a price tag on that."[39] Both Ladysmith and Juanes put on exciting shows but for different reasons. Both fit the program's current slogan, "Great Music, No Limits."

Both also fit the expansive spirit of the new studio space and venue, which Lickona sees as a way for *Austin City Limits* "to take what has been a platform and a showcase for great music on television all these years and make it [in the venue] a platform and a showcase for great music 365 days a year for a live audience in addition to the audience that watches it on television."[40] The program's geographic and historical grounding, then, becomes an asset, by affording a logical harmony to new physical realities for *Austin City Limits* and to many different musical sounds. As Freddy Fletcher put it, "Austin's really not a big genre kind of town …there's so many different kinds of music this town is known for and that's kind of the beauty of it. You can hear anything here."

[10]

LIKE HELIOTROPES
TOWARD THE SUN

I tore open the red-and-white Netflix envelope containing a full-hour DVD recording of Fats Domino on *Austin City Limits* from way back in Season 12 (1987). I was 17 when the episode first aired. By then Fats Domino reigned as a rock-and-roll legend with more than three decades behind him. He was a classic borderland figure in American popular music, and that night he performed in Studio 6A with joie de vivre.

By the second song, his cover of the standard "My Blue Heaven," sweat streamed from his hairline down into his collar. More than once Domino grabbed a big white cloth from the top of the piano to mop his forehead with one hand while the other hand kept the steady boogie-woogie beat. *Austin City Limits* floor manager Ray Lucero, with the show since the pilot, recalled this as the only taping they ever did without air conditioning. "And this was in the summertime when we did it.... He likes to sweat. So we had the audience sweat with us."[1] About a third of the way into the performance, he invited audience requests. "Walking to New Orleans," "Blueberry Hill," and other famous Domino numbers followed in short order.

Behind the *Austin City Limits* scenes, Terry Lickona worked for years to get Fats Domino on the show. In fact in the early 1980s Domino, who never cared to leave New Orleans much, backed out of a show for which tickets had already been printed.[2] Lickona persisted. He sent *Austin City Limits* tapes of other musical lions like Carl Perkins, Jerry Lee Lewis, and Roy Orbison to Domino's home.[3] He spoke with people close to Domino, including his son Antoine Jr. Quint Davis, director of the New Orleans Jazz and Heritage Festival, talked to Domino on Lickona's behalf. Lickona met him following a San Antonio gig, "but came away with nothing more than an autograph." Finally he sat down with him in a Las Vegas hotel room after another show. As Lickona put it, "Between Fats's New Orleans jive and my Yankee-by-way-of-Texas blather, somehow there emerged a deal for him to do the show."

Watching Fats Domino on the DVD, he moves the same way I remember seeing in clips from the 1950s when he was a young man. He sits face forward at the piano, tending a lick, only to swing in a sudden wide arc to the right just in time to deliver the next lyric. Domino sings into the microphone, stationed a bit farther away than seems convenient, a fact that causes him to lean slightly back at the same time it positions him and his smile in a line of direct communication with the audience. Fats Domino's steady, rhythmic movements and his flat-out charisma dominate the televised concert despite the crowd of other musicians on stage with him. Thirteen in all traveled with him to Texas: two rotating drummers, two guitarists, and seven horn players, including longtime band members Lee Allen and Herbert Hardesty, and, on trumpet, Dave Bartholomew, the New Orleans–based producer, co-writer, and bandleader who helped shape Domino's rollicking sound.

This was a historic *Austin City Limits* episode even when it first aired—a showcase for a legendary performer whose stage vigor remained intact decades after his first success. The currents of significance had deepened still more by the time the DVD arrived in my mailbox in 2012. Rumors of Domino's death and his dramatic rescue via helicopter during Hurricane Katrina in 2005 had renewed appreciation for his legacy. These events led to spots on NPR, the release of an album he had recorded in 2000 titled *Alive and Kickin'*, an invitation to headline the New Orleans Jazz and Heritage Festival, and a visit from President Bush to replace the National Medal of Arts Award lost in the flood.[4] They also inspired new demand for the *Austin City Limits* episode and its hour-long, uninterrupted look at the musical luminary in action before an intimate live audience.[5] Where else would such a performance have been preserved? The Fats Domino episode today still remains a treasure of latter-twentieth-century American popular music.

The same might be said for many *Austin City Limits* episodes over the years. An impulse to archive follows naturally on the heels of institutional recognition, and *Austin City Limits* people have been preserving the show's history in a more deliberate way in recent years. That job often falls to Michael Toland, whose title on his business card reads "Manager of National Productions" at KLRU but he also serves as archivist. His daily tasks range from assisting in production to collecting and cataloging the bits and pieces that accumulate. This includes books, albums, bootleg recordings, and "anything that anybody who goes into a museum might have any interest in at all, even if it's just one person."[6] Ray Davies's handwritten set list, for example, which once hung on Toland's office wall, now goes in the collection. The thank you note Leonard Cohen wrote after he first saw his own episode aired goes there. Things get missed along the way. Perhaps they should have kept the box where Neko Case packed homemade cookies and brownies, a thank-you gift for the *Austin City Limits* staff.

The process of digitizing the entire collection of tapes from past *Austin City Limits* episodes began in 2011, an impetus for the station to acquire its own system for managing massive digital assets.[7] Whether the end results of this work will be publicly available in some form or another for the *Austin City Limits* opus is not clear. Regardless of its ultimate destiny, the collection amounts to a substantial archive of popular music performances over the past four decades.

Watching the Fats Domino show and, really, any other episode, demonstrates the simultaneous fixed and flexible nature of *Austin City Limits*. Just like other recorded media, *Austin City Limits* captures a moment in a constant and changing flow of music, and suspends it, preserves it for us to examine over and over again like a rock plucked from a streambed. Popping the disc into the DVD player brings to my television screen the same sequences of images and sounds broadcast to living rooms across the country 20-odd years before: Fats Domino, circa 1987, in an Austin time capsule.[8] Yet the environment into which that episode replays changed a great deal between 1987 and 2012. The historical resonance of Fats Domino deepened over the intervening decades, as did the historical resonance of *Austin City Limits*.

If, as Ed Bailey reflected, the practical "processes of how we do the show"—its basic televisual approach and attention to audio— remain continuous with the past, so much else has changed. In order to survive, the show evolved from its original focus on Austin's progressive country scene to an eclectic mix of musical genres that includes Miranda Lambert and The Decemberists, Raphael Saadiq and Joanna Newsom, all in the same season (Season 37, 2011–2012). Time brought waves of technology upgrades for equipment, along with external changes like the especially grueling and concentrated taping schedule that now flanks the *ACL* Festival weekend. *Austin City Limits* was flexible enough to roll with changing tastes, trends, and technologies, yet fixed enough to remain recognizable by audiences.

Television itself changed, too. *Austin City Limits* no longer takes what Bailey termed the "analog approach": "you make a product here, you send it to them, it's programmed somewhere in America, and three hundred stations say, 'We'll put this on at this time, you people come watch it, it's on at 7 o'clock.'"[9] *Austin City Limits* now circulates differently. It still broadcasts on PBS stations across the country but also streams episodes or real-time performances online. It intuitively skates a line between local ambience and national relevance, a line that is source, model, and reflection

Figure 10.1 Unveiling the plaque designating *Austin City Limits* a music landmark by the Rock and Roll Hall of Fame.

for the national (or even international) relevance of the city of Austin, the *ACL* Music Festival, and now the *ACL* Live venue. Signaling its own recognition of constant motion, station KLRU hired Tom Gimbel to bring wide-ranging music industry experience—performing, marketing, managing his record label—to a newly created position as General Manager for *Austin City Limits* in March 2011.[10]

Finally, audiences changed. The conceptual structures for understanding how this music relates to that, manifested in genre terms and other words for talking about music, never remain stable. People do not remain stable. I do not experience Fats Domino the same way in 2012 as I did in 1987. The DVD's arrival to my Atlanta mailbox creates new opportunities for me to engage the performance and, thus, new opportunity for meaning. Perhaps I mean opportunity for new meaning. Both are at work the moment I push "play."

Austin City Limits at this point exists on the level of ideas. It is a festival that draws 75,000 people to Austin's Zilker Park to spend three days taking in the 130-plus acts over a weekend or two in the fall. Twitter feeds, blogs, and YouTube pages track both show and festival. The 2011 lineup included Stevie Wonder and Kanye West, Coldplay and Arcade Fire, Damian Marley and Cee Lo, the Preservation Hall Jazz Band and The Warrior Gospel Band. The venue, *ACL* Live at the Moody Theater, now serves as television studio for recording episodes 50 or so days per year, and otherwise draws a wide range of acts: Dwight Yoakum, Cedric the Entertainer, Owl City, Buddy Guy, Joanna Newsom, Chicago, and Alejandro Escovedo and the Sensitive Boys were all on the summer schedule in 2011.

Ed Bailey takes it all in together to say that *Austin City Limits* has become "a place to discover—a place to have a real good music

experience."[11] That "place" takes on an ever-more-fluid definition: the TV, the computer screen, the mail order DVD, the "app,"
the live venue, the annual music festival, and so on. As an idea,
the shape and potency of *Austin City Limits* get tested in ways no
one could have imagined in 1975: by people watching the program
live, on TV, on a computer screen propped on a back porch chair,
or people visiting the festival, or people attending an event at the
Moody, or people surfing one of several websites, posting to a blog,
buying a DVD, "liking" it on Facebook, and so on.

As to future possibilities, who knows? Would it work for small
tours to travel under the banner *"Austin City Limits* Presents"?
They could feature indie bands, or roots artists, or country musicians or whatever genre might work in a particular market, playing
smaller venues within a limited geographic area. Would it work to
tape shows in 3D and then show them in movie theaters?[12] That
might connect right back to the show's emphasis from the very
start on a deliberate and natural approach to conveying musical
performance on screen. Ideas like these could take on a life of
their own, as did festival and venue. Or they might go the same
way as the notion of an *Austin City Limits* beer that surfaced in the
late 1990s.[13]

The changes that pushed the transformation of *Austin City
Limits* from television show to musical experience stuck because
they were rooted in something real. That real something includes
the city and the show's PBS context. The show, festival, venue, and
other aspects of the *Austin City Limits* experience connect to one
another via, as Lickona stated, "the quality of the presentation and
the authenticity of the music."[14] Above all, they work because of
the people involved. They work because each idea bore the potential to "develop it without getting too crazy or spreading ourselves
too thin."[15] The people who make *Austin City Limits* happen still

have fun doing it, which counts for a lot. In Lickona's words, "the fun that we have and the fun the artists have is contagious, and that's part of the experience people have."[16]

In 2009, 30 years after he produced his first season, Terry Lickona talked to me about how his job had changed. Many of his duties remain the same: booking the talent, hiring the core staff, working with KLRU to manage the budget, overseeing the editing process, matching artists with one another for single episodes, and determining the order of episodes for a given season. Yet deeper elements of the enterprise changed profoundly.

> My whole perspective about the show, my philosophy about the show has had to change because I now have to think of it as more than just a television show. Now, for one thing, there is this huge history behind the show, which certainly didn't exist thirty years ago when I started. And that history, the legacy, certainly has an impact on everything the show stands for and will continue to stand for in the years to come.[17]

Terry Lickona's primary concern remains the television program *Austin City Limits*. Yet "managing that legacy" now takes place within a context that includes so much more than it once did. The festival, the venue, and all the related undertakings carry a potential "to rejuvenate the show yet again, to take it to a higher level."[18] Just as they shore up one another, they all underscore Austin's claim to musical verve, one that artists, media, business people, and politicians worked on throughout the years since *Austin City Limits* began.

Twelve seasons constituted an impressive run in 1987, the year Fats Domino's episode first aired. By 2012 the achievement was singular in US television: a long-standing program devoted to

Figure 10.2 Some of the people who help make *Austin City Limits* happen participate in a panel moderated by the Rock and Roll Hall of Fame's VP for Education and Public Programs, Dr. Lauren Onkey. From right to left: Onkey, David Hough, Gary Menotti, Terry Lickona, Leslie Nichols, Jeff Peterson, and Emily Joyce.

portraying live musical performance, uninterrupted by commercials or hosts, on the air for nearly four decades. In some ways the show's growing prominence mirrors the chic prestige that accrued to the city of Austin, particularly as the "Live Music Capital of the World." Austin meant more by then, and *Austin City Limits* exemplified its home city's reputation for supporting musicians and for bending the ears of music lovers toward it, like heliotropes toward the sun.

POSTLUDE

When Juanes returned to record a second episode on June 4, 2013, this time from the Moody venue, his performance streamed live over the YouTube channel for "AustinCityLimitsTV." It was a one-time event, beginning at 8:00 p.m. CST, 9:00 p.m. EST. I marked it on my calendar and, when the time came, sat down to watch from a back porch in Atlanta. I no longer normally catch *Austin City Limits* at the day and time my local PBS affiliates schedule it—and not only because they aim for midnight or after. I watch it when I have a moment, sometimes through the TV monitor and sometimes on the laptop. The Juanes concert came as another take on experiencing *Austin City Limits*.

It was not yet an episode because Menotti and editor Dan Martaus had not yet made it one. (Certainly they will pause over one of the few times Juanes spoke to the audience in English: "When I was here seven years ago, I didn't really understand what it meant. But now I look back at this [gesturing to the skyline backdrop], and I say 'F***.' I'm on *Austin City Limits*, man.") Watching this felt fleeting like a concert or a festival because it was over when it was over. Yet it took place 950 miles (or 1,530 kilometers) from my house, and came to me via screen. I dwelt in between live and mediated in a novel way and recalled Freddy Fletcher telling me when it was still under construction that the Moody would make this kind of technology available at the flip of a switch. In this way technology created access to an experience of aesthetic pleasure, nuanced in novel ways yet grounded in the core identity of *Austin City Limits*.

It happened again the next week, when Michael Kiwanuka performed live on June 10, 2013 for an episode to be broadcast in November. These forays into live streaming were becoming a regular part of the taping cycle for *Austin City Limits* by Season 39. I watched, knowing the whole set would be edited down to 30 minutes for the final airing. I imagined Gary Menotti calling the camera cues behind the scenes, guessed at certain shots that might need to be cleaned up a bit, anticipated which songs might work best and which might be cut for the final episode. Mostly I once again enjoyed the chance to see the unbroken performance, there on my television monitor, which this time I had hooked up along with the stereo speakers to my laptop in anticipation of the event. I occasionally monitored the tally showing the number of viewers simultaneously sharing the moment. Mediated and live at the same time, I thought of this newest layer of potential meaning for *Austin City Limits*. I would need to watch the schedule and return to what I thought was a bygone impulse to mark my calendar for a musical media event.

My perspective comes very much from the outside. How much more striking must it all seem from inside? Terry Lickona described one of those moments that must come with some regularity in recent years for longtime *Austin City Limits* staffers. Lickona had ducked out for a few hours on the taping day, October 30, 2013, for the band known as Portugal. The Man.[1] Long before the booking, Lickona had committed to co-chair a charity function, so he turned over his normal duties of welcoming the audience and making pre-show announcements to producer Jeff Peterson. On the way back, 30 minutes or so into the taping, Lickona paused at a red light and used his phone to log on to the YouTube site where the program streamed. "There I was sitting in my car at a stoplight in South Austin," he told me, "watching *Austin City Limits* LIVE on my iPhone. It was a bit surreal."[2]

ACKNOWLEDGMENTS

This project began with my participation on a panel at the American Culture Association/Popular Culture Association joint meeting in San Antonio, Texas, in March 2004. *Austin City Limits* won the Ray and Pat Browne Award for Outstanding Contributions to American Culture. The ceremony surrounding this award included a panel of scholars reflecting on the show's significance. The research I undertook in preparation for the event sparked my interest in pursuing a larger project about *Austin City Limits*. The more I thought about the way the show's trajectory syncs up with other stories within its orbit—PBS and the city of Austin, and also the (r)evolution of media that has radically altered the way audiences relate to popular music—the more I thought "Someone should write a book about that." Ten years later, here we go. I thank the organizer Ray Merlock and fellow panel participants for getting things rolling.

That panel was the first time I met Terry Lickona, the executive producer and guiding force behind *Austin City Limits* since Season 4, and Ed Bailey, Vice President for Brand Development at public television station KLRU. Both participated as commentators and respondents. During the decade since that meeting, they demonstrated openness, patience, graciousness, willingness to help, and enthusiasm for the project at every turn. The book never would have happened had they not believed in its value and trusted my voice to tell a version of this remarkable program's story. I am grateful for the hours they spent talking, and for the welcome they gave whenever I announced I was swinging into town for yet another foray into their world. I hope to have done the tale justice.

My thanks also goes to everyone else working on the show. I learned a great deal from people who took time out for formal interviews. In addition to Lickona and Bailey, they include Jeff Peterson, Bill Arhos, Michael Toland, Maury Sullivan, Robert Moorhead, Doug Robb, Ray Benson, Scott Newton, Ray Lucero, Walter Olden, Gary Menotti, and David Hough. (An extra special note of gratitude goes to Scott Newton for the beautiful cover shot.) I spoke with others more casually or, in some cases, admired them from afar. There is a unique dynamic at *Austin City Limits* and I consider it my privilege to have observed their work as a team fueled by a shared love and appreciation for music, by an intuitive grasp of their individual roles in the overall production, and by mutual goodwill. As associate producer Leslie Nichols commented during an interview, not with me, people tend to stay on the show because it feels like a family. That positive vibe is obvious to a bystander. Along these lines, I thank Leslie Nichols, Dick Peterson, Emily Joyce, Sharon Cullen, David Kuipers, Augie Meyers, and Steven Durr. I thank Bill Stotesbury and Tom Gimbel, as well, for permissions and support.

Research on the show led me to conversations with others involved in related pursuits. I thank Freddy Fletcher and Tim Neece for taking time to talk about the new venue when it was still under construction. I also thank Charlie Jones and Lisa Hickey for generosity with their time and perspective at C3 Presents. I thank Marie Rowell for giving me a place to stay when I came to town and for sharing musical experiences as well as breakfast burritos. Old friends hold a special place in the heart. As a side note, I thank everyone who makes delicious breakfast burritos in Austin, Texas.

I thank my excellent colleagues in the Agnes Scott College music department whose collegiality, friendship, and support are very dear and make our collective undertaking a pleasure: Whitney Brown, Qiao Solomon, Jason Solomon, David D'Ambrosio, Elise Eskew-Sparks, Dawn-Marie James, and so many others. My students fuse every day (almost!) with an extra boost of energy and inspiration, and I am grateful to them for it. Other colleagues past and present, including Susan Dougherty, have supported my work whether they realize it or not and I also thank colleagues who read portions of the work or otherwise (sometimes unwittingly) helped give me a boost. These include members of the Agnes Scott "Last Fridays" faculty group, including Peggy Thompson and David Williams, and, in less direct but equally significant ways, the "Germany trip" fellow faculty travelers. I also appreciate the students who assisted with transcribing interviews over the years including Rachel Cook, Tatyana Adams, Brittany Balfour, Lauren Welch, Ashley E. Williams, and others.

Agnes Scott College offered invaluable support for completing this project. I especially thank President Elizabeth Kiss, former Vice President for Academic Affairs Carolyn Stefanco, and former and current Associate Vice Presidents for Academic Affairs Jim Diedrick and Kerry Pannell. Members of the Professional Development Committee approved funding for regular research trips to Austin, and recommended the sabbatical release time necessary to corral this project into a coherent narrative. The library staff members have been wonderful as well, including Director Elizabeth Bagley and Resa Harney in Technical Services, Debbie

Adams for so many interlibrary loan requests, and Casey Long, research librarian extraordinaire.

Along the way I have encountered colleagues at other institutions who have offered expertise and assistance. Among them, I owe a big debt of gratitude to Dr. Maggie Rivas-Rodriguez at the University of Texas School of Journalism for sharing the work of her students in the Oral History project from 2007. Lauren Goodley, archivist at the Southwestern Writers Collection, the Wittliff Collections, at Texas State University in San Marcos was a great help. Steve Weiss, Curator of the Southern Folklife Collection and Sound and Image Library at the Wilson Library, University of North Carolina–Chapel Hill, helped move the project along at an early phase. I also thank Stephanie Malmros, Head of Archives, along with other library staff members at the The Dolph Briscoe Center for American History at the University of Texas in Austin. Late-inning thanks go to Jessi Cape, Cassandra Pearce and other helpful staffers at the *Austin Chronicle*.

I deeply appreciate Suzanne Ryan and her editorial team at Oxford University Press, including Adam Cohen, Lisbeth Redfield, Caelyn Cobb, Molly Morrison, Douglas Nicholas, along with Lauren Hill, and others I fear I missed. Anonymous readers for the proposal and early chapters helped clarify directions for the project, and the final reader raised important points that ultimately strengthened the end result and fine-tuned its direction. My thanks further goes to colleagues scattered afield who have participated on panels related to this research, including Travis Stimeling, Jason Mellard, Karl Hagstrom Miller, Jim Deaville, and others. I deeply appreciate feedback and support from Mark Slobin, James Akenson, and Bill Malone. More generally, I have grown from interactions with fellow academics at gatherings that include the Society for American Music, the International

Country Music Conference, the Post 45 Conference, and the Society for Ethnomusicology.

Above all, I thank the friends and family who attended the unfolding of this project, and me during it, offering encouragement, critique, editorial skills, insight, a laugh or two, and many other passing daily kindnesses and love that help a person "keep keeping," as Georgia native and godfather of soul James Brown might have said. They include Mike and Judy Lynn (a double mention to Mike for his mighty editorial eye). They also include loved ones Anne Widiger, Eric and Sara Widiger, Cody Widiger, Janice Laird, Megan and Jessica Byrnes-Laird, other Lairds, Millers, Winterrowds, and Widigers far and wide.

Brandon Laird contributed to this project in more ways than a person can name—from offering editorial suggestions at many different stages to, more generally, having my back in this passage through life. He finished his own book during the time I worked on this one (*Future Great*, published on Amazon for Kindle readers and apps—Brandon Laird, aka Ezra Camp). I also thank Henry and Zoey for the up-close-and-personal, day-in-and-day-out joys they bring to my world. They are tremendous people, and I am fortunate to be in their association, having birthed them and all.

NOTES

Introduction

1. "Sense of discovery" was the phrase used to characterize the show by Jim Henke, a former *Rolling Stone* music editor and Vice President for Exhibitions and Curatorial Affairs at the Rock Hall from 1994–2012, during the second panel celebrating the occasion of *Austin City Limits'* induction into the Rock and Roll Hall of Fame, October 1, 2009; "good music" comes up regularly in discussions of *Austin City Limits,* for instance with Ed Bailey, interview with the author, Austin, TX, July 7, 2010; digital recording.

Chapter 1

1. The term "scene" had been in widespread use among journalists at least since they first tried to describe jazz culture. In the 1990s, the "scene" entered academic parlance describing the phenomenon of people creating a sense of community around a distinct musical style or genre. Local music scenes could include particular music venues, record shops, or independent record labels, and commonalities shared among the scene's members: dress, patois, political views, a particular kind of recreational drug, and so forth. The idea of the "scene" relates to the notion of a subculture, but it is looser conceptually; it implies fluidity in how deeply participants can move in and out of identification with the scene. Scenes might have strong ties to a particular location, like the 1990s Seattle scene or the 1980s Athens scene, or they might operate more generally, as in the rave scene, punk scene, or bluegrass scene.

2. Bill Malone, *Country Music, U.S.A.*, rev. ed. (Austin: University of Texas Press, 1985), 395; also referenced in Chris Smith, *101 Albums That Changed Popular Music* (New York: Oxford University Press, 2009). Also see Travis Stimeling, *Cosmic Cowboys and New Hicks: The Countercultural Sounds of Austin's Progressive Country Music Scene* (New York: Oxford University Press, 2011), which includes musical analysis of some key recordings associated with Austin's progressive country scene from the late 1960s to the mid-1970s.

3. *Texas Folk & Outlaw Music at the Kerrville Festival*, Edsel Records/Adelphi Records, EDCD 352, 1983; 1992.

4. Murphey, *Cosmic Cowboy Souvenir*, Beverly Hills, CA: A&M, SP-4388, 1973.

5. This way of characterizing it comes from Barry Shank, *Dissonant Identities: The Rock and Roll Scene in Austin, Texas* (Hanover, NH: University Press of New England, 1994). Also see Karl Hagstrom Miller, "That's Right, You're Not from Texas: Exploring Some Outside Influences on Texas Music," *The Journal of Texas Music History* 1, no. 2 (fall 2001): 5–16.

6. Miller writes, "This perceived difference between Texas culture and the popular culture of the nation was essential to how music in Texas was promoted, categorized, and talked about by people both inside and outside the state" (ibid., p. 7). He further notes that Lomax very deliberately directed his "cowboy informants" about the specific kind of material he desired to collect—material that supported a particular picture of Texas cowboy culture as isolated.

7. Eddie Wilson, interview with Thomas Fawcett and Jazmin Cavazos, April 12, 2007, Austin; *Austin City Limits* Oral History Project Records, 2007, Dolph Briscoe Center for American History, The University of Texas at Austin; DVD copy in author's files.

8. N.a., "Music: Groover's Paradise," *Time* (September 9, 1974), accessed April 22, 2011;http://www.time.com/time/magazine/article/0,9171, 904125-2,00.html.

9. David McGee, "What Is Progressive Country?" *Record World* (March 6, 1976): 4; in Archie Green Collection, box labeled AG 80, Papers—Cosmic 1, Southern Folklife Collection, The Wilson Library, University of North Carolina at Chapel Hill.

10. Bill Arhos, email to the author, August 7, 2011.

11. Bill Arhos, interview with the author, July 12, 2007, Austin; digital recording.

12. Arhos interview. Round Rock is a Texas town about 20 miles from Austin.

13. David Hough, interview with the author, July 12, 2007, Austin; digital recording.

14. Terry Lickona, personal email to the author, September 6, 2012.

15. This holds true today. It was apparent when I emailed a local PBS affiliate in Atlanta about moving the show back to prime time, a spot lost due to fee

structure changes at PBS in the 1990s (see chapter 5, "A Place to Discover Music"). The polite response came from the station's director, who said that "most rock/country/pop music performance programs that we air in Prime do not generate much of an audience," a state he chalked up to the possibility that "concerts on television are no longer unique or it could be that the accessibility of concert footage on YouTube may dilute the product." Email from Dustin Lecate, Director of Television, PBA 30, October 9, 2009. His thinking justifies and updates a long-standing institution of doubt among television programmers about live music's appeal. Never mind the steady stream of programs like "60s Pop, Rock & Soul: My Music" and other live PBS tributes to music whose popularity peaked a half-century before and whose performers sometimes seem barely up to the task of cycling through the set list of old favorites.

16. Claudia Perry, "15 Years of 'Austin City Limits,'" *The Houston Post*, January 25, 1990, D-1. She also mentions these, along with USA's *Night Flight*, "the first cable show that aired live performances" from 1980 to 1988, as examples of all the shows *ACL* outlasted.

17. See Joe Nick Patoski, *Willie Nelson: An Epic Life* (New York: Little, Brown and Company, 2008), 267–8.

18. Wilson interview with Thomas Fawcett and Jazmin Cavazos; emphasis mine.

19. See Joe Frolik, "Keeping in Tune with 'Austin City Limits,'" *Austin American-Statesman*, October 1, 1978; "Austin City Limits" vertical file, Dolph Briscoe Center for American History.

20. Stimeling, 34.

21. Arhos interview.

22. Patoski, 268.

23. Arhos interview.

24. Scott Newton, interview with the author, July 13, 2007, Austin; digital recording; newspaper clippings from over the years also quote Arhos's well-traveled quip.

25. See Patoski, 28; and Willie Nelson with Bud Shrake, *Willie: An Autobiography* (New York: Simon and Schuster, 1988), 59–60; also mentioned in Bob St. John, "Willie Nelson—A Real Man," *Scene*, August 10, 1975, 13; clipping in Bill Arhos Collection of *Austin City Limits* [VF Arhos/ACL 886], Southwestern Writers Collection, The Wittliff Collections, Texas State University.

26. For more discussion on the significance of Willie Nelson within the broader progressive country scene, see Stimeling, *Cosmic Cowboys*.

27. John T. Davis, "Expanding the Borders of 'Austin City Limits,'" *Austin American-Statesman*, July 30, 1982, C1; Bill Arhos Collection of *Austin City Limits* [VF Arhos/ACL 886-2]. Davis also mentions the *Time* magazine story.

28. Neil Reshen, the lawyer who represented Willie Nelson and others in this era, made the comparison during an interview with music scholar Don Cusic. See "Neil Reshen: Riding Herd on the New Breed," *Record World*, March 6, 1976, 6.

29. "Shine On Country Soul: Pop," *New York Times*, May 19, 1974, 148; in ProQuest Historical Papers: *The New York Times* (1851–2008). Also referred to in St. John, 10.

30. Wayne Slater, "'Austin City Limits' Moves to Changing Beat," *Dallas Morning News*, February 10, 1985, 1A; clipping in Bill Arhos Collection of *Austin City Limits* [VF Arhos/ACL 888-2].

31. Ibid., 32A.

32. Larry Williams, "Willie Nelson Was Limit," *Memphis Commercial Appeal*, March 24, 1975.

33. Ibid.

34. Letter from Bill Arhos, dated April 25, 1975; in Bill Arhos Collection of *Austin City Limits*.

35. Jennifer C. Lena and Richard A. Peterson, "Classification as Culture: Types and Trajectories of Music Genres," *American Sociological Review* 73 (2008): 711.

36. St. John, "Willie Nelson—A Real Man," 8.

Chapter 2

1. Gwen Gibson, "Stars Shine Bright in 'Austin City Limits,'" *Savannah Morning News*, August 22, 1994; in Bill Arhos Collection of *Austin City Limits* [VF Arhos/ACL 887-5], Southwestern Writers Collection, The Wittliff Collections, Texas State University.

2. See Hugh Cullen Sparks, "The Stylistic Development and Compositional Processes of Selected Solo Singer/Songwriters in Austin, Texas," PhD dissertation, University of Texas, 1984, 42. Sparks writes about Holland "calling the style 'country-folk-rock-science-fiction music' in 1969, at which time Steve Fromholz expanded the label to 'country-folk-rock-science-fiction-gospel-gum-blue-grass-opera music." (Also see Travis Holland, *Texas Genesis: A Wild Ride Through Texas Progressive Country Music 1953–78, With Digressions* [Austin: B.F. Deal Publishing Co., 1978], 86.)

3. Joe Nick Patoski, *Willie Nelson: An Epic Life* (New York: Little, Brown and Company, 2008), 309. See the Introduction and chapter 1 for more discussion of Nelson's mid-1970s significance.

4. David Hough, interview with the author, July 12, 2007, Austin; digital recording.

5. Letter from Bill Arhos, dated April 25, 1975; in Bill Arhos Collection of *Austin City Limits*.

6. Undated press release by Ken Waggoner, Radio and Television, Folder 77, *Austin City Limits*, Southern Folklife Collection, The Wilson Library, University of North Carolina at Chapel Hill; quotes in this and the following paragraph come from the same document.

7. Archie Green, "Austin's Cosmic Cowboys: Words in Collision," in *"And Other Neighborly Names": Social Process and Cultural Image in Texas Folklore*, ed. Richard Bauman and Roger D. Abrahams (Austin: University of Texas Press, 1981), 188.

8. Ibid.

9. Undated press release from Season 1, in Radio and Television, Folder 77, *Austin City Limits*, Southern Folklife Collection.

10. Karl Hagstrom Miller, "That's Right, You're Not from Texas: Exploring Some Outside Influences on Texas Music," *The Journal of Texas Music History* 1, no. 2 (fall 2001): 7, 10.

11. Press release titled "Rusty Weir [sic] Brings Good Time Music to AUSTIN CITY LIMITS," in Bill Arhos Collection of *Austin City Limits*.

12. Undated press release from Season 1, in Radio and Television, Folder 77, *Austin City Limits*, Southern Folklife Collection. Incidentally, Jim Reeves's hometown of Galloway, near Carthage, is really more eastern than southern Texas; the two regions are distinct in many ways.

13. Sparks, p. 53, makes a similar observation when he describes the song as "an ideal representation of the loose, rock- and folk-inspired, tongue-in-cheek approach to music" that typified the scene.

14. Ben Ratliff, "Guitarist Clarence Gatemouth Brown Dies at 81," *New York Times*, September 12, 2005, accessed August 21, 2012; http://www.nytimes.com/2005/09/12/arts/music/12brown.html?_r=1.

15. From a SPC-4 Program Series proposal from February 1978; document located in the "cage" material at station KLRU, since relocated to the Rock and Roll Hall of Fame in Cleveland.

16. Joel Williams, "Musical show projects intimate setting," unidentified newspaper clipping, n.d., in Bill Arhos Collection of *Austin City Limits* [VF Arhos/ACL 886-11].

17. Joe Frolik, "Keeping in Tune with 'Austin City Limits,'" *Austin American-Statesman*, October 1, 1978; clipping in VF Austin City Limits, Dolph Briscoe Center for American History, The University of Texas at Austin.

18. Memo from Barbara Van Dyke to Bill Arhos, dated July 5, 1978; in Bill Arhos Collection of *Austin City Limits*.

19. For an insightful exploration of progressive country in Austin, see Travis Stimeling, *Cosmic Cowboys and New Hicks: The Countercultural Sounds of Austin's Progressive Country Music Scene* (New York: Oxford University Press, 2011).

20. See Barry Shank, *Dissonant Identities: The Rock and Roll Scene in Austin, Texas* (Hanover, NH: University Press of New England, 1994).

21. Clifford Endres, *Austin City Limits* (Austin: The University of Texas Press, 1987), 28, 34–5. Arhos stepped into the producer's role during Season 2, then Charles Vaughn.

22. Bruce Scafe, telephone interview with Talor Schaddalee, April 20, 2007; *Austin City Limits* Oral History Project Records, 2007, Dolph Briscoe Center for American History; recording in author's files.

23. It was understandable that Charles Vaughn might have been unnerved by trying to accomplish both directing and producing duties all at the same time; his need to shift some production duties elsewhere helped open the door for Terry Lickona to prove himself, which he did, to say the least. See Endres, 39.

24. Hough interview.

25. Joe Frolik, "Keeping in Tune ..."

26. Hough interview.

27. Press release dated Nov. 7, 1980; in VF Austin City Limits, Dolph Briscoe Center for American History.

Chapter 3

1. Gary Menotti, conversation with the author and camera operator Doug Robb, KLRU, July 10, 2007; digital recording.

2. Doug Robb, interview with the author, July 10, 2007, Austin; digital recording.

3. Robert Moorhead, interview with the author, July 13, 2007, Austin; digital recording.

4. Robb interview. Subsequent quotes by Robb come from this interview unless otherwise noted.

5. Michael Toland, email to the author, April 15, 2013.

6. Moorhead interview. In the new space, a remote-controlled track-mounted camera that runs along the bottom of the first balcony covers the shots once taken by the Wizard-of-Oz crane. On the floor, a second smaller crane adds yet more visual variety.

7. Walter Olden, interview with the author, July 13, 2007, Austin; digital recording.

8. David Hough, interview with the author, July 12, 2007, Austin; digital recording.

9. Rush Evans, "Bob Wills and His Texas Playboys," *Discoveries* (1998), accessed June 28, 2010; http://www.texasplayboys.net/Biographies/bobwillsbio.htm.

10. Hough interview. Subsequent quotes by Hough come from this interview, unless otherwise noted.

11. Pete Szilagyi, "KLRU Survives in Network World," *Austin American-Statesman*, September 2, 1990, 1.
12. Elianne Halbersberg, "Austin City Limits," *Mix* 33, no. 3 (March 2009): 30.
13. Ibid.
14. David Hough, email message to the author, January 6, 2012.
15. Clifford Endres, *Austin City Limits* (Austin: University of Texas Press, 1987), 59.
16. Bill Arhos, interview with the author, July 12, 2007, Austin; digital recording.
17. Ibid.
18. Scott Newton, interview with the author, July 13, 2007, Austin; digital recording.
19. This photo, along with many other great Newton shots, is found in Terry Lickona and Scott Newton, eds., *Austin City Limits: 35 Years in Photographs* (Austin: University of Texas Press, 2010), n.p.
20. In Lickona and Newton, n.p.
21. Newton interview.
22. Robert Albers, "Quality in Television From the Perspective of the Professional Programme Maker," in Sakae Ishikawa, ed., *Quality Assessment of Television* (Luton, Bedfordshire, UK: University of Luton Press, 1996), 141.

Chapter 4

1. See Jim Yardley, "Austin Journal; A Slogan Battle Keeps Austin Weird," *New York Times*, December 8, 2002, accessed May 2, 2013; http://www.nytimes.com/2002/12/08/us/austin-journal-a-slogan-battle-keeps-austin-weird.html. Also see Joshua Long, *Weird City: Sense of Place and Creative Resistance in Austin, Texas* (Austin: University of Texas Press, 2010).
2. See Todd M. Thompson, "A Sound Divided: The Battles of Musical Space in Austin, Texas," MA thesis, University of Texas, 2010, 4–5; Thompson recounts the story of the near riot during a 1978 performance by The Huns at an Austin club called Raul's; see also Barry Shank, *Dissonant Identities: The Rock and Roll Scene in Austin, Texas* (Hanover, NH: University Press of New England, 1994), 104.
3. Scott Newton, interview with the author, July 13, 2007, Austin; digital recording.
4. Undated press kit sheet titled "Austin City Limits VI, Suggested Spot Copy"; in Country Music Foundation archives, Country Music Hall of Fame® and Museum, Nashville, Tennessee; photocopy.
5. John T. Davis, "Expanding the borders of 'Austin City Limits,'" *Austin American-Statesman*, July 30, 1982, C3; Bill Arhos Collection of *Austin City Limits* [VF Arhos/ACL 886-2], Southwestern Writers Collection, The Wittliff Collections, Texas State University.

6. Ibid.; Davis likewise quotes director Gary Menotti as saying that "'Austin City Limits' has always been strongly country-oriented and Austin music isn't anymore."

7. Terry Lickona, interview with the author, August 11, 2011, Austin; digital recording.

8. Undated press kit sheet titled "Austin City Limits IX, Suggested Spot Copy"; in Country Music Foundation archives; photocopy.

9. *Stevie Ray Vaughan and Double Trouble: Live from Austin, Texas,* DVD, Epic Music Video, EVD 50130, 1989; 1995.

10. Undated press sheet titled "Austin City Limits Season 10, Suggested Spot Copy"; in Country Music Foundation archives; photocopy.

11. Troupe Earnest Gammage Papers, 1981–1992, Dolph Briscoe Center for American History, University of Texas at Austin; document dated November 25, 1986.

12. Ibid.; later bumper sticker comes from Gwen Gibson, "Texas City Is 'Music to Your Ears,'" *Savannah Morning News,* August 21, 1994; in Bill Arhos Collection of *Austin City Limits* [VF Arhos/ACL 887-5].

13. KLRU's ambition to be in the minority of producing stations within the PBS system continues to develop; in the words of a more recent reporter, KLRU aims to be "the Austin station carrying PBS programming rather than the PBS outlet in Austin." See Louis Black, "Page Two: Seasons Change, and So Do We," *Austin Chronicle,* October 6, 2006, accessed April 10, 2013; http://www.austinchronicle.com/columns/2006-10-06/408182/.

14. Gammage Papers; document dated November 16, 1989.

15. Gibson, "Texas City is 'Music to Your Ears.'"

16. Gary Dinges, "Study: Austin's creative sector has $4.35 billion economic impact," *Austin American-Statesman,* March 12, 2012, accessed May 2, 2013; http://www.statesman.com/news/business/study-austins-creative-sector-has-435-billion-ec-1/nRmBW/.

17. See Resolution 910829-46; accessed June 24, 2011. http://www.austintexas.gov/edims/document.cfm?id=24298.

18. Ed Bailey, interview with the author, July 7, 2010, Austin; digital recording. The city specified high-density affordable housing, the construction of hotel rooms to attract the "green" industry of convention business, and a non-profit as priorities for the space. At one point, the construction plans included a relocated children's museum, in addition to the new home for *Austin City Limits.* The museum later backed out of the project.

19. Pete Szilagyi, "KLRU Survives in Network World," *Austin American-Statesman,* September 2, 1990, 1.

20. Robert Moorhead, interview with the author, Austin, July 13, 2007; digital recording.

21. Letter from Bill Arhos to Chet Atkins, February 1, 1990. Bill Arhos Collection of *Austin City Limits* (Box 3, Folder 5).

22. Brad Buchholz, "Beyond the Cosmic Cowboys," *Dallas Morning News*, February 25, 1990, 1C; clipping in VF Austin City Limits, Dolph Briscoe Center for American History.

23. Claudia Perry, "15 Years of 'Austin City Limits,'" *The Houston Post*, January 25, 1990, D-1.

24. Michael Point, "Loud and Clear: 'Austin City Limits' Shows U.S. variety of Music for 15 Years," *Austin American-Statesman*, January 19, 1990; in VF Austin City Limits, Dolph Briscoe Center for American History.

25. Lee Nichols, "'ACL's' 16th year packs momentum," *Austin American-Statesman* January 17, 1991, 9; in VF Austin City Limits, Dolph Briscoe Center for American History.

26. Bill Arhos, interview with the author, July 12, 2007, Austin; digital recording.

27. In that same February 1, 1990, letter to Chet Atkins, Arhos wrote, "I saw the Emery show on TNN where you were talking about taking up the banjo. We just did some stuff with Bela Fleck…who seems to have taken that instrument farther than its inventor might have imagined. When they asked Franklin Roosevelt how many strings a banjo has, he said, 'Five too many!' I'm afraid the guitar is going to be enough challenge to last me a lifetime." Bill Arhos Collection of *Austin City Limits* (Box 3, Folder 5).

28. Don McLeese, "'ACL' Still Hasn't Reached Its Limits," *Austin American-Statesman*, January 14, 1993; in *Austin City Limits* files, Barker Texas History Collection, Dolph Briscoe Center for American History.

29. N.a., "Will Stations Leave 'Limits' Behind?," *Austin American-Statesman*, January 12, 1996; in *Austin City Limits* files, Barker Texas History Collection.

30. Terry Lickona, interview with the author, July 9, 2007, Austin; digital recording.

31. Don McCleese, "A Mecca for Musical Mavericks," *Billboard* 110, no. 21, May 23, 1998, accessed December 14, 2011; Business Source Complete.

32. Pierre Bourdieu, *On Television*, trans. Priscilla Parkhurst Ferguson (New York: The New Press, 1998), 20.

33. This concept threads through Bourdieu's writings. See, for example, *On Television*, 43, where he discusses the "symbolic capital" of the newspaper *Le Monde* as both source and explanation for its authority. See also Bourdieu, *The Field of Cultural Production: Essays on Art and Literature*, ed. Randal Johnson (New York: Columbia University Press, 1993). Occasionally, he draws a line between symbolic capital as that which springs from institutional or critical recognition and cultural capital more as recognition among other "producers" within a given "field." More often he uses cultural capital interchangeably with symbolic capital, both of which contrast with financial profitability or "economic capital." See also Bourdieu, *Distinction: A Social Critique*

of the Judgement of Taste, trans. Richard Nice (Cambridge, MA: Harvard University Press, 1984), 53–4, or 114–15, for example.

Chapter 5

1. Freddy Fletcher and Tim Neece, interview with the author, July 8, 2010, Austin; digital recording. Fletcher and Neece originally said 65 feet during our interview, which occurred during construction, but Fletcher later confirmed the adjusted number in a personal email to the author.
2. Jon Pareles, "'Austin City Limits': Live Music, No Frills," *New York Times*, May 19, 1989, accessed December 14, 2011; LexisNexis.
3. Press release in the "cage" at station KLRU, since relocated to the Rock and Roll Hall of Fame in Cleveland.
4. Steve Johnson, "Back to the Roots: Channel 11 Pays a Rare Visit to the Fine Musicians Of 'Austin City Limits,'" *Chicago Tribune*, June 12, 1998, accessed December 11, 2012; http://articles.chicagotribune.com/1998-06-12/features/ 9806120393_1_austin-city-limits-robert-earl-keen-son-volt.
5. Psychologists and linguists, too, know that categories are a fundamental way by which people make sense of the world. As one scholar puts it, "Albums, songs, and performers that fit into more than one category can be rendered irrelevant but also produce opportunities for new identities." For a consideration of the power of categories, see George Lakoff, *Women, Fire, and Dangerous Things: What Categories Reveal About the Mind* (Chicago: University of Chicago Press, 1987). The quote comes from Jennifer C. Lena, *Banding Together: How Communities Create Genres in Popular Music* (Princeton, NY: Princeton University Press, 2012), 153.
6. Marybeth Gradziel, "Austin City Limits," *The Austin Chronicle*, March 25, 1988, 1; in VF Austin City Limits, Dolph Briscoe Center for American History, The University of Texas at Austin.
7. Ibid.
8. Ed Bailey, personal email communication, January 24, 2007.
9. Steve Johnson, "Back to the Roots."
10. N.a., "Will Stations Leave 'Limits' Behind?," *Austin American-Statesman*, January 12, 1996, n.p.; clipping in *Austin City Limits* files, Eugene C. Barker Texas History Collection, Dolph Briscoe Center for American History.
11. Diane Holloway, "Updated but downsized," *Austin American-Statesman*, January 30, 1998.
12. Ed Bailey, interview with the author, September 20, 2006, Austin; cassette recording.
13. Bill Arhos, interview with the author, July 12, 2007, Austin; digital recording.
14. Document dated April 16, 1998; in boxes in KLRU "cage."

15. Clifford Endres, "Redneck Music and Public TV," *American Way*, February 15, 1989, 60; clipping in VF Austin City Limits, Dolph Briscoe Center for American History, The University of Texas at Austin.
16. Ibid., *Austin City Limits* (Austin: University of Texas Press, 1987), 59.
17. Arhos interview, 2007.
18. Press release dated March 10, 1998, in boxes in KLRU "cage"; the quoted parts were in all caps in the original document.
19. Document in KLRU "cage."
20. Bailey interview, 2006.
21. Ibid.
22. Arhos interview, 2007.
23. Bailey interview.
24. Fabian Holt, *Genre in Popular Music* (Chicago: University of Chicago Press, 2007), 46, also notes negative stereotypes associated with the term "country music," particularly for fans of the later genre of Americana.
25. John T. Davis, "Austin City Limits," *Austin American-Statesman XLent*, January 12, 1995, n.p.; clipping in *Austin City Limits* files, Eugene C. Barker Texas History Collection.
26. See Diane Holloway, "Upstaged? New PBS Series from NY Prompts Discussion of Future of Long-Running KLRU Staple 'Austin City Limits,'" *Austin American-Statesman*, June 28, 1997.
27. Press materials from KLRU records; my thanks go once again to Michael Toland for sharing this material electronically.
28. Arhos interview. Jim Henke made a similar observation during the panel celebrating the occasion of *Austin City Limits'* induction into the Rock and Roll Hall of Fame, October 1, 2009.
29. Bailey, telephone conversation, September 25, 2009.
30. Terry Lickona, interview with the author, September 20, 2006, Austin; digital recording; and idem, July 9, 2007; and idem August 11, 2011.
31. Archie Green, "Austin's Cosmic Cowboys: Words in Collision," in *"And Other Neighborly Names": Social Process and Cultural Image in Texas Folklore*, ed. Richard Bauman and Roger D. Abrahams (Austin: University of Texas Press, 1981), 188.

Chapter 6

1. Marc Raboy, "Introduction: Public Service Broadcasting in the Context of Globalisation," in *Public Broadcasting for the 21st Century*, ed. Raboy (London: University of Luton Press, 1995), 13.
2. Bourdieu makes a parallel observation about politics when he says, "Above all, time limits make it highly unlikely that anything can be said." His statement could easily apply to music. See Pierre Bourdieu, *On Television*, trans.

Priscilla Parkhurst Ferguson (New York: The New Press, 1998), 15. As far as exceptions go, my mind turns, for example, to Prince's mid-1980s performances on the Grammys or on the American Music Awards as memorable moments of televised music. The age of cable television during the 1990s opened new potential to expand what might be called the network television paradigm, notably MTV's *Unplugged* series. Yet that program's aura sprang in part from that very exceptionalism: it ran counter to the type of musical material upon which *MTV* first made its name and to the commercialized ambiance of *MTV* as a whole. Its concerts featured artists out of their normal performance modes, and audiences experiencing a "real" encounter with musicians on a media channel otherwise overtly devoted to commercial flash. Nirvana's 1993 performance remains a tremendous one whose poignancy was underscored by Kurt Cobain's death soon thereafter. Its singularity also supports the argument that *Austin City Limits* carved out a unique space. All the while, cable in general and its digital successors reverted back to the standard disruptive, commercial-driven network TV paradigm, finding the alternatives financially unsustainable.

3. See Robert Vianello, "The Power Politics of 'Live' Television," *Journal of Film and Video* 38 (Summer 1985): 26–40, for a discussion of the way "live" production served as a strategy for the large networks to maintain commercial dominance over independent television producers.

4. Live television broadcasts fell in the United States "from 81.5 percent in June 1953 to 26.5 percent in 1961"; see John Mundy, *Popular Music on Screen: From Hollywood Musical to Music Video* (Manchester: Manchester University Press, 1999), 181; also 207. Also, Vianello, 35, notes that 75% of prime-time programming was pre-recorded by 1957.

5. Vianello, 7, distinguishes videotape from earlier use of film.

6. The idea of television's "liveness" or sense of presence and "being there" winds throughout Jeffrey Sconce, *Haunted Media: Electronic Presence from Telegraphy to Television* (Durham, NC: Duke University Press, 2000); see, for example, 16, 130, and 173, where he suggests that the medium's "'liveness' appears to be a function of the technology itself," due to the continuous stream of unbroken images in contrast to the movement by frames that characterizes film. Also see Jane Feuer, "The Concept of Live Television: Ontology as Ideology," in *Regarding Television: Critical Approaches—An Anthology*, ed. E. Ann Kaplan (Frederick, MD: University Publications of America, 1983), 14.

7. See John A. Ferejohn and Roger G. Noll, "An Experimental Market for Public Goods: The PBS Station Program Cooperative," *The American Economic Review* 66, no. 2 (May 1976): 270. They analyze the value of PBS's newly introduced system for decentralizing programming decisions known as the Station Programming Cooperative (SPC). So self-evident was the notion

that the "average number of 'takes' per printed scene" was a measure of worth that it was mentioned along with "number of scenes filmed on location" in an offhanded, parenthetical definition of "production quality."

8. Martie McGuire made this observation as a member of an artists' panel put together on the occasion of *Austin City Limits'* induction into the Rock and Roll Hall of Fame, October 1, 2009.

9. Letters between Vern Moreland and Bill Arhos, dated February 22, 1983 and March 1, 1983; in Bill Arhos Collection of *Austin City Limits*, Southwestern Writers Collection, The Wittliff Collections, Texas State University.

10. Karl Pallmeyer, "The Maestro in the Control Booth," *Austin Business Journal*, July 7–13, 1995, 6; clipping in Bill Arhos Collection of *Austin City Limits* [VF Arhos/ACL 886-7].

11. Transcript of interview with B.B. King on September 19, 1995; folder labeled "ACL 21 Interviews," located in the "cage" material at station KLRU, since relocated to the Rock and Roll Hall of Fame in Cleveland; accessed on October 1, 2009.

12. Lickona, interview with the author, August 11, 2011, Austin; digital recording.

13. Author's notes during taping for Cat Power in Studio 6A.

14. Elianne Halbersberg, "Austin City Limits," *Mix* 33, no. 3 (March 2009): 32.

15. See, for example,Walter Kellogg Towers, *Masters of Space* (New York and London, 1917); Edward A. Herron, *Miracle of the Air Waves: A History of Radio* (New York: Julian Messner, 1969), 86.

16. For example, see Mildred Steffans, "The Case for Visualized Music in Television," *Telescreen: For the Arts of Television* (Spring 1945): 9. Despite some cringe-worthy predispositions and prejudices ("although we are limiting ourselves here to a discussion of good music, even 'swing' can be visualized with tremendous effect"), her ponderings about new art forms merging music and visual imagery came before television's future was clear and its central position in domestic life fully imagined.

17. See Murray Forman, " 'One Night on TV Is Worth Weeks at the Paramount': Musicians and Opportunity in Early Television, 1948–55," *Popular Music* 21, no. 3 (2002): 249–76.

18. Forman, 255.

19. Quoted in Forman, 268.

20. Mundy, 5.

21. See Mundy.

22. Ibid.

23. This must have been what another British media scholar, Keith Negus, had in mind when he suggested that "musicians and television personnel" alike tend "to treat television as if it were a neutral lens, rather than a transformative medium that can redefine, or develop innovative types of, musical

NOTES

performance." See Keith Negus, "Musicians on Television: Visible, Audible and Ignored," *Journal of the Royal Music Association* 131, Part 2 (2006): 314.

24. Ibid., 320. This discussion of music on the television "small screen" relates to the recent phenomenon of live streaming major operatic and dramatic stage performances in "big screen" movie theaters, an in-between-live-and-mediated experience initiated by the New York Metropolitan Opera's "Live at the Met" series and taken up by London's "National Theatre Live" events. See Leslie A. Wade, "The London Theatre Goes Digital: Divergent Responses to the New Media," *Theatre Symposium* 19 (2011): 54–68; and Paul Heyer, "Live from the Met: Digital Broadcast Cinema, Medium Theory, and Opera for the Masses," *Canadian Journal of Communication* 33 (2008): 591–604. The discussion occurs in sources for more general readership as well; see, for example, Jonathan Mandell, "Putting the 'Theatre' in 'Movie Theatre,'" *American Theatre* (May/June 2011): 66–9; or Thomson Smillie, "Onstage and Online: will live opera, orchestra, and ballet in Louisville survive the rise of simulcasts and digital downloads from the world's best performing-arts companies?" *Louisville Magazine* 61, no. 11 (November 2010): 80–3. Scholars of theater and art likewise question the extent to which apprehension of the radical nature of the modern digital age "moves our historical investigations beyond the binary of the live and recorded." See, for example, Sarah Bay-Cheng, "Theater Is Media: Some Principles for a Digital Historiography of Performance," *Theater* 42, no. 2 (2012): 40.

25. Alan O'Connor, ed., *Raymond Williams on Television: Selected Writings* (London: Routledge, 1989), 82; in Stuart Laing, "Raymond Williams and the Cultural Analysis of Television," *Media, Culture and Society* 13 (1991): 157.

26. In my mind this equates to "authenticity" via "neutrality," in Negus's sense.

27. Keith Negus, 320, suggests that *any* televised live music is by its nature unrealistic. I suppose the same could be said on some level for any television at all.

28. Doug Robb, interview with the author, July 10, 2007, Austin; digital recording; subsequent quotes from Robb in this chapter come from the same interview.

29. Robert Moorhead, interview with the author, July 13, 2007, Austin; digital recording. Subsequent Moorhead quotes in this chapter come from the same interview.

30. Use of the word "aura" refers to Walter Benjamin, "The Work of Art in the Age of Mechanical Reproduction," in *Art in Modern Culture: An Anthology of Critical Texts*, ed. Francis Frascina and Jonathan Harris (London: Phaidon Press Limited, 1992). On p. 299 he makes his well-traveled assertion that "that which withers in the age of mechanical reproduction is the aura of the work of art."

31. Laing, 164. Writing in 1974, Williams suggested that television's greatest value rests in its potential "for genuine and direct communication," and

commented that "a man talking and showing us his work is among the best television there is" (in Laing, 169 and 158 respectively). In general, Laing urges television scholars to focus less attention on Williams's amorphous concept of "flow" and more attention to his other powerful ideas.

Chapter 7

1. See Lynn Spigel, "Introduction," in *Television After TV: Essays on a Medium in Transition,* ed. Spigel and Jan Olsson (Durham: Duke University Press, 2004), 1–2. She frames her discussion of "transformations in the practice we call watching TV" within what she calls the "digital culture of 'convergence'"; see also in the same volume John Caldwell, "Convergence Television: Aggregating Form and Repurposing Content in the Culture of Conglomeration," 41–74. Similar terms pop up throughout scholarship on the contemporary media environment.

2. See Caldwell, "Convergence Television," for discussion of how the structure of the commercial television industry discourages risk-taking, at the same time it has introduced a newly defined "vertical integration" of power and re-segregation of programming content.

3. John Mundy, *Popular Music on Screen: From Hollywood Musical to Music Video* (Manchester: Manchester University Press, 1999), 201.

4. See Caldwell, "Convergence Television," 61–5, for discussion of "stunting" strategies that typify commercial television, particularly during "sweeps" season, the time frame for measuring audience shares that determine a program's sponsorship rates.

5. Spigel, "Introduction," 2; Caldwell and Uricchio also comment on this phenomenon in the same volume. See William Uricchio, "Television's Next Generation: Technology/Interface Culture/Flow," in Spigel and Olsson, 163–82.

6. As media scholar Laurie Ouellette suggests, PBS programs are "ascribed value precisely because they appeared in public television's selective cultural environment." She points out that "even programs that do not on [sic] automatically convey prestigious cultural associations" like "nature specials and *Sesame Street*" participate in this meaning structure. See Laurie Ouellette, *Viewers Like You? How Public TV Failed the People* (New York: Columbia University Press, 2002), 218.

7. Scott Newton, interview with the author, July 13, 2007, Austin; digital recording. Subsequent quotes from Newton in this chapter come from the same interview.

8. Ed Bailey, interview with the author, September 20, 2006, Austin; cassette recording.

9. Public broadcasting stations today would do well to infuse a similar injection of energy and freshness, a thought that follows hearing an advertisement

for rehashed Andy Williams Christmas specials as the big draw on my local affiliate station's evening programming.

10. PBS website, accessed October 10, 2012, http://www.pbs.org/about/corporate-information/.

11. See section titled "The TV Freeze," in Frank J. Kahn, ed., *Documents of American Broadcasting*, 4th ed. (Englewood Cliffs, NJ: Prentice-Hall, 1984), 179–90.

12. See "The 'Vast Wasteland,'" in Kahn, 207–17; on p. 211, he states that, like a sales figure, a rating shows "how many people saw" a program, but "does not reveal the depth of the penetration, or the intensity of reaction, and it never reveals what the acceptance would have been if what you gave them had been better—if all the forces of art and creativity and daring and imagination had been unleashed."

13. See "President Johnson's Message to Congress," H.R. Doc. 68, 90th Congress, 1st Session, February 28, 1967, in Kahn, 250–3. These ideas languished for a decade and a half between the FCC's initial action in 1952 and the 1967 act.

14. "President Johnson's Message," in Kahn, 252.

15. Undated press release by Ken Waggoner, Radio and Television, Folder 77, *Austin City Limits*, Southern Folklife Collection, The Wilson Library, University of North Carolina at Chapel Hill.

16. Charges of elitism cyclically surface in the context of debates about public spending priorities and PBS, despite the fact that the portion of the federal budget devoted to public broadcasting is relatively miniscule. In 1999, only 11.6 percent of the PBS system was federal money. See Ouellette, 6. The debates always bring public broadcasting critics to the fore, who often stake their points on populist grounds that the highbrow content of PBS does not serve the common people who fund it, a point backed up by Nielsen statistics. Other critics sometimes caricature the collection of independent public broadcasting stations as unwieldy little fiefdoms battling for territory, i.e., airwaves, or now, broadband. For example, James Day characterizes US public television as conceptually "blurred in a babel of diverse aims" and functioning through a "hydra-headed structure of competing authorities." See *The Vanishing Vision: The Inside Story of Public Television* (Berkeley: University of California Press, 1995), 5, accessed October 18, 2012; http://publishing.cdlib.org/ucpresse-books/view?docId=ft7x0nb54q&chunk.id=d0e36&toc.id=&toc.depth=1&brand=ucpress&anchor.id=bkd0e84#X.

17. Box 1, "ACL 18 Proposal" folder; in the "cage" material at station KLRU.

18. Holloway, "Upstaged? New PBS Series from NY Prompts Discussion of Future of Long-Running KLRU Staple 'Austin City Limits,'" *Austin American-Statesman*, June 28, 1997.

19. Communications scholar Marc Raboy, for instance, contrasts the goals of different media outlets in exacting terms: "Public broadcasting aims to touch people, to move them, to change them. Private broadcasting, by nature, aims to put them in the mood to consume and, above all, to consume more of what private broadcasting has to offer." See "Introduction: Public Service Broadcasting in the Context of Globalisation," in *Public Broadcasting for the 21st Century*, ed. Raboy (London: University of Luton Press, 1995), 13. Communications professor Michael Tracey paints the opposition dramatically: "In a public system, television producers acquire money to make programmes. In a commercial system they make programmes to acquire money." See Tracey, *The Decline and Fall of Public Service Broadcasting* (New York: Oxford University Press, 1998), 18. His British spelling "programmes" underscores the fact that much public broadcasting scholarship is Eurocentric and misses some distinctive aspects of the US situation.

20. Ouellette, 6. Later, Ouellette points out that the practice of corporate sponsorship initiated by Nixon's funding refusal effectively set the conditions for the sustained targeting of PBS programming toward an upper-class, highly educated, white viewing audience; it established the avoidance of "Middle America" programming that presumably were the populist grounds for his objections in the first place.

21. I find George Lakoff's concept of radial (as opposed to classical) categories helpful here; their boundaries are neither rigid nor are their characteristics mutually exclusive. They include common features, like sponsors and demographics, yet these features occupy varying distances from the core of each category. See *Women, Fire, and Dangerous Things: What Categories Reveal About the Mind* (Chicago: The University of Chicago Press, 1987).

22. See Carolyn Anderson's discussion of the late 1990s documentary *Hawaii's Last Queen*, for instance, in "Contested Public Memories: Hawaiian History as Hawaiian or American Experience," in *Television Histories: Shaping Collective Memory in the Media Age*, ed. Gary R. Edgerton and Peter C. Rollins (Lexington: The University Press of Kentucky, 2001), 149.

23. Diane Werts, "How to Wow a Critic," *Newsday (Queens Edition)*, July 12, 1998.

24. Raboy, 13, explains the difference between long-term audience reach versus short-term audience share. Ouellette, 5, again cites 'image surveys' that indicate people perceive public television as "more educational, serious, tasteful, and important than commercial television." Even on commercial TV, certain sponsors avoid programs that project low standards, or a bottom-feeder atmosphere; some, for example, "won't go near certain of the reality shows because they find them not an appropriate environment." Louis Chunovic, "Advertisers Face Reality," *Television Week*, January 27, 2003, cited in Spigel, "Introduction," 25 n. 6.

25. Author's notes, Rock Hall panel.

26. Bill Arhos, interview with the author, July 7, 2007, Austin; digital recording.

27. From an April 22, 1992, memo from Terry Lickona to the staff; located in the "cage" material at station KLRU, Box 1, "ACL 18 Proposal" folder, since relocated to the Rock and Roll Hall of Fame in Cleveland.

28. Gwen Gibson, "Stars Shine Bright in 'Austin City Limits,'" *Savannah Morning News*, August 22, 1994; in Bill Arhos Collection of *Austin City Limits* [VF Arhos/ACL 887-5], Southwestern Writers Collection, The Wittliff Collections, Texas State University.

29. Spigel, "Introduction," 5.

30. Caldwell, "Convergence Television," 54–5.

31. Ouellette, 217.

32. Author's notes from October 1, 2009 panel discussions in honor of *Austin City Limits'* designation as a "landmark" by the Rock and Roll Hall of Fame.

33. Author's notes from Miranda Lambert taping during Summer 2005.

34. As Ouellette, 218, puts it, PBS (as a brand) situates them together in a "meaning system," which creates coherence between them.

35. Caldwell, "Convergence Television," 57.

36. See Richard Middleton's discussion of the mid-1950s music industry shakeup, which resonates with the Internet revolution, in *Studying Popular Music* (Milton Keynes, Buckinghamshire, UK: Open University Press, 1990), 85; also see Mundy, 180.

37. Caldwell, "Convergence Television," discusses the ways people interact with characters from *Dawson's Creek* in ways separate from the show itself.

38. Uricchio, 222.

39. See Jostein Gripsrud, "Broadcast Television: The Chances of Its Survival in a Digital Age," in *Television After T.V.*, ed. Spigel and Olsson, 218–19, for discussion of how cognitive psychology may explain why "people tend to watch a rather limited set of channels even if given many alternatives."

40. Uricchio, 168–77, discusses the "radical displacement of control" these devices (and the vast array of modern media choices that inspired them) represent, in contrast to greater audience control sparked by earlier technology of the Remote Control Device.

41. See Jeffrey Sconce, *Haunted Media: Electronic Presence from Telegraphy to Television* (Durham, NC: Duke University Press, 2000), 185, for a discussion of theories (originating from Christian Metz and others) of television spectatorship as typified by "fleeting and intermittent attention" (the glance) versus the absorbed viewing that typifies film spectators (the gaze). John Caldwell takes issue with this presumed duality between the experience of film and TV viewing, arguing that this contrast ignores the possibility of absorbed and "entranced" television viewers. I take his point to heart that TV audiences assume different levels of attentiveness, depending on their own nature

or the nature of the programming; I also appreciate the caution about over-generalizations of any sort. Still, he fails to convince me to throw out the fundamental distinction wholesale. My own experience in a darkened cinema does contrast with my experience before my living room television in ways that assure the continued health of the film industry. More significantly, his critique of "the myth of distraction" neglects to account for the dominating presence of commercial interruptions within the majority of television viewing. The "glance" still rings true for me, even more so in the new media environment. See John T. Caldwell, *Televisuality: Style, Crisis, and Authority in American Television* (New Brunswick, NJ: Rutgers University Press, 1995), 25–7.

42. I am reminded of Julian Johnson's treatise on the disconnection between modern media and long-form musical content of a symphonic work, particularly his comparison of effects of, for instance, a phone interruption on listening to a Beethoven symphony and engaging in lovemaking. Neither lends itself well to divided attention. See Julian Johnson, *Who Needs Classical Music? Cultural Choice and Musical Value* (New York: Oxford University Press, 2002). Use of the word "flow" can describe this aesthetic immersion, but I have avoided it here since, in a different sense, television scholars rely on "flow" to describe the nature of television as experienced by its audience.

Chapter 8

1. Lisa Hickey, interview with the author, Austin, July 8, 2010; digital recording. Subsequent quotes from Hickey in this chapter come from the same interview.
2. Hudson's chicken cones were such a hit at the *ACL* Music Fest that the restaurant owner eventually opened two smaller satellite businesses that specialize in the dish. Jeff Blank, "Our Story," accessed June 4, 2013; http://www.mightycone.com/our_story.html.
3. Lickona noted that the *ACL* Music Festival is one of the nation's top five festivals as part of an educational panel for the induction of *Austin City Limits* into the Rock and Roll Hall of Fame, October 1, 2009.
4. Terry Lickona, interview with the author, Austin, July 9, 2007; digital recording.
5. Michael Corcoran, "A Dynamic Duet for 'Austin City Limits,'" *Austin American-Statesman*, September 17, 2004.
6. Ed Bailey, interview with the author, Austin, September 20, 2006; cassette recording.
7. Bailey, phone conversation with the author, September 25, 2009.
8. Michael Corcoran, "'Austin City Limits' Festival Promoter Savors the Sweet Sound of Success," *Austin American-Statesman*, September 19, 2003.

9. Charlie Jones, interview with the author, Austin, July 8, 2010; digital recording. Jones said he saw potential for another big music festival, "a great opportunity for that in the city of Austin.... With the demise of Aqua Fest, the city
was missing a big summer celebration of the music culture." Subsequent
quotes from Jones in this chapter come from the same interview. Attendance
figure comes from a report by Pat Kaufman to the Austin Music Industry
Council; minutes included in the Troupe Earnest Gammage Papers, 1981–
1992, Dolph Briscoe Center for American History, University of Texas at
Austin.
10. Bailey interview, 2006.
11. Corcoran, "Austin City Limits"; according to this source CSE acquired
Middleman in August 2001.
12. Ibid.
13. Bailey interview, 2006.
14. Bailey, phone conversation.
15. Jones interview. According to the *Austin City Limits* Music Festival event summary, produced by C3 Presents for its sponsors, 20% of 2009 festival-goers
earned yearly salaries greater than $100,000; another 12% earned above
$75,000. 26% of 2009 Austin festival goers had graduate education; 55% had
earned a college degree. The 2008 numbers are similar, with 21% of patrons
earning over $100,000 and 22% percent with post-grad education. By con-
trast, Lollapalooza attracted 9% of its audience from the over-$100,000
income bracket and 18% with graduate degrees of some kind.
16. By contrast, forerunners like Lilith Fair and OzzFest traveled to different
locations. The same company that stages the *ACL* Music Festival expanded
a few years later by reinvigorating Lollapalooza; among other changes,
they redefined the once-traveling festival into a "destination," this time in
a Chicago city park. Their success in Austin "got us in the door in the city of
Chicago," as Jones reflected during our interview.
17. Lickona interview, 2007. Subsequent quotes by Lickona in this chapter come
from this interview unless otherwise indicated.
18. Sociologist Sarah Thornton dubs the term "subcultural authenticity" in her
book on club cultures, which fits as well as "cultural capital" to convey the
hip ambiance of *ACL*. See Sarah Thornton, *Club Cultures: Music, Media,
and Subcultural Capital* (Hanover: University Press of New England, 1996).
Whereas the DJ guaranteed the subcultural authenticity for a particular
dance club scene, *ACL*'s subcultural authenticity comes from its attachment
to a specific place, both geographic and mediated. Thornton, 60, writes, "By
orchestrating the event and anchoring the music in a particular place, the DJ
became a guarantor of subcultural authenticity." Its anchor, in Thornton's
sense, is key to understanding both the longevity of *Austin City Limits* on
television and, by extension, the rapid success of the festival.

19. Bailey interview, 2006.
20. Bailey phone conversation.
21. Ibid.
22. Technically, the station hires Terry Lickona as executive producer and budget manager through his production company called LickonaVision, which also employs several members of the *Austin City Limits* team. In terms of practical operation, so fluid are everyone's efforts that it is impossible to distinguish from the outside who works for KLRU and who works for LickonaVision during a taping.
23. Corcoran, "A Dynamic Duet"; Attendance Breakdown for the First Year Comes from Corcoran, "Austin City Limits."
24. David Hough, interview with the author, Austin, July 12, 2007; digital recording.
25. The arrangement for formal collaboration on booking *Austin City Limits* came initially as a surprise to Lickona, who learned of it after the deal was done. See Corcoran, "A Dynamic Duet."
26. Bailey interview, 2006.
27. Ibid.
28. Hough interview.
29. Bailey interview, 2006.
30. Jones interview.
31. Now it reads "Austin Parks Foundation Presents ..."
32. In years since, college sports have aired in the shade tent, also known as Rock Island Hideaway.
33. I borrowed the phrase "symbolic economy" from David Grazian, "The Symbolic Economy of Authenticity in the Chicago Blues Scene," in *Music Scenes: Local, Translocal, and Virtual*, ed. Richard A. Peterson and Andy Bennett (Nashville: Vanderbilt University Press, 2004), 31–47.

    Grazian discusses the subjective experience of authenticity based on a number of symbols that collectively take on meaning within the Chicago blues scene. The idea of collective meaning relates to *Austin City Limits* in some parallel ways.
34. That aspect of the phenomenon of music applies to other settings as well. Music events can engender feelings of connection, community, and belonging among participants. Thornton, p. 111, talks about the "spontaneous affinity" felt among youthful members of British club subcultures, underscoring social aspects of music's appeal.
35. It fits a framework Dean MacCannell first hypothesized back in the mid-1970s as key to understanding the depth of tourist experiences. Festivals fall into a category of "cultural productions" that include: "programs, trips, courses, reports, articles, shows, conferences, parades, opinions, events, sights, spectacles, scenes and situations" whose value lies in the "quality and quantity of

experience they promise." See *The Tourist: A New Theory of the Leisure Class* (New York: Schocken Books, 1976), 23–24. Although MacCannell's work is nearly as old as *Austin City Limits*, it remains relevant because few others have considered "destination attractiveness," a term from tourism studies, from a sociologist's or anthropologist's point of view. In particular, his theoretical concept of "site sacralization" resonates with what has occurred in Austin, and with *Austin City Limits* as a key part of that. Republished in 1989 and again in 1999, MacCannell's *The Tourist* continues to find application and relevance in scholarly work across disciplines. Recent examples include both specific and general studies such as Linda Joyce Forristal, Dawn Gay Marsh, and Xinran Y. Lehto, "Revisiting MacCannell's Site Sacralization Theory as an Analytical Tool: Historic Prophetstown as a Case Study," *International Journal of Tourism Research* 13 (2011): 570–82, accessed October 10, 2013, doi: 10.1002/jtr.830; or Arthur Asa Berger, "Tourism as a Postmodern Semiotic Activity," *Semiotica* 183, no. 4 (2011): 105–19, accessed October 12, 2013, doi 10.1515/semi.2011.006; or Michaela Benson, "Living the 'Real' Dream in *la France profonde*? Lifestyle Migration, Social Distinction, and the Authenticities of Everyday Life," *Anthropological Quarterly* 86, no. 2 (spring 2013): 501–25.

36. See Dean Rindy, "Country Karma," *The Texas Observer*, April 14, 1972, 17–19; in Archie Green Collection, box labeled AG 81, Southern Folklife Collection, The Wilson Library, University of North Carolina at Chapel Hill. Organizers expected the event to draw 60,000 people but it drew only half that many.

37. Undated press release from 1975 by KLRN employee Toni Frazer, who writes about the 3rd annual Fourth of July picnic at Liberty Hill, Texas, attended by around 70,000 people; in Radio and Television, Folder 77, *Austin City Limits*, Southern Folklife Collection.

38. Hickey interview. As she put it, "some music fans…are more engaged than anything you've ever seen.… I think that's rare and that's what people [sponsors] are buying: the quality of the people, not the quantity."

39. Jones interview.

40. Hickey interview.

41. Jones interview.

42. Ibid.

43. Hickey interview.

44. Thornton, 143–4. Drawing on Baudrillard's reflection on "hyperreality," A. A. Berger likewise suggests that "images are now more important than the reality they capture." See Berger, 113.

45. Again, the overlap between live and mediated experience is a topic addressed in scholarship on the recent occurrence of movie theater "events" featuring, for instance, live streaming of theater and opera performances including London's "National Theatre Live" and New York's "Live at the Met" series.

Chapter 9

1. Ray Lucero, interview with the author, August 9, 2011, Austin; digital recording. Late in 2013 KLRU donated the old crane camera to the Americana Music Association where it may someday become part of a museum exhibit; Terry Lickona, personal communication, November 4, 2013.

2. Jeff Peterson, interview with the author, July 13, 2007, Austin; digital recording.

3. Author's notes, panel celebrating the occasion of *Austin City Limits'* induction into the Rock and Roll Hall of Fame, October 1, 2009, Austin.

4. Clifford Endres, "Redneck Music and Public TV," *American Way*, February 15, 1989, 60; clipping in VF Austin City Limits, Dolph Briscoe Center for American History, The University of Texas at Austin.

5. Quoted in Ibid., 54; I extend a special note of appreciation to Ms. Lana Ader, editorial assistant at American Way/Celebrated Living/AA Nexos magazines for scanning a copy of this piece so I could confirm wording of a quote.

6. Undated press release by Ken Waggoner, Radio and Television, Folder 77, *Austin City Limits*, Southern Folklife Collection, The Wilson Library, University of North Carolina at Chapel Hill.

7. David Hough, interview with the author, July 12, 2007, Austin; digital recording.

8. Bill Arhos reported the rumor that former first lady Laura Bush was once a volunteer behind the beer table at *Austin City Limits*, but I have been unable to verify that.

9. Terry Lickona, email communication to the author, February 17, 2014; a version of the story also came up in Bill Arhos, interview with the author, July 12, 2007, Austin; digital recording.

10. Arhos interview.

11. Arhos recalled this incident to journalist and writer John T. Davis; seeDavis, "Expanding the Borders of 'Austin City Limits,'" *Austin American-Statesman*, July 30, 1982, C3; in Bill Arhos Collection of *Austin City Limits* [VF Arhos/ACL 886-2], Southwestern Writers Collection, The Wittliff Collections, Texas State University.

12. Wayne Slater, "'Austin City Limits' Moves to Changing Beat," *Dallas Morning News*, February 10, 1985, 1A; clipping in Bill Arhos Collection of *Austin City Limits* [VF Arhos/ACL 888-2]. Ely quote is from Brad Buchholz, "Beyond the Cosmic Cowboys," *Dallas Morning News*, February 25, 1990, 6C; clipping in VF Austin City Limits, Dolph Briscoe Center for American History.

13. Kinky Friedman, *Kinky Friedman: Live from Austin Texas*, directed by Gary Menotti, 59 min., New West Records, B000RF1QNI, 2007.

14. Among other places, I found this referred to in John T. Davis, *Austin City Limits: 25 Years of American Music* (New York: Billboard Books, 2000), 79,

where Lickona indicated that Kristofferson headed to the roof to watch the storm. Other versions of this well-circulated story often put Lickona in the position of leading the audience out of darkness; it makes a great story, but Lickona clarified the actual facts of the incident via personal communication. I admit my partiality to the legendary version.

15. Hough interview.

16. Peterson interview.

17. Terry Lickona, interview with the author, August 11, 2011, Austin; digital recording.

18. Ibid.

19. Ibid.

20. Reflections on the bleachers saga come from Lickona, August 11, 2011 interview.

21. Michael Toland, interview with the author, August 10, 2011, Austin; digital recording.

22. Ray Lucero, interview with the author, August 9, 2011, Austin; digital recording.

23. Lucero interview.

24. Leslie Nichols commented on this tradition during an interview by Emily Wilkinson, April 11, 2007, Austin; *Austin City Limits* Oral History Project Records, 2007, Dolph Briscoe Center for American History; DVD copy in author's files. I still fondly remember tasting Kuipers's African ground nut stew on one of these occasions.

25. Terry Lickona and Scott Newton, eds., *Austin City Limits: 35 Years in Photographs* (Austin: University of Texas Press, 2010), n.p.; also, Michael Toland interview.

26. Leslie Nichols, interview by Emily Wilkinson.

27. Ibid.

28. Lucero interview. Also Michael Toland, interview with the author, August 10, 2011, Austin; digital recording.

29. Lickona interview, 2011. Subsequent quotes in this paragraph come from here as well.

30. Freddy Fletcher, with Tim Neece, interview with the author, July 8, 2010, Austin; digital recording.

31. Quoted in Ellen Lampert-Greaux, "Beyond City Limits," *Live Design* 45, no. 6 (August 2011): 23; Steven Durr Designs, LLC, is based in Nashville.

32. Quoted in Lampert-Greaux, 22; he went on to say that "we successfully moved them into a much larger new space, not leaving the intimacy behind and still making it sound as they intended on TV, radio, and live [*sic*]." Later in the piece, he explains why he relies more on dialogue than on musical sounds to test and shape his acoustic space: "It is harder to fool people with

the spoken word.... Once you get the vocal sound correct, it is easy to fill in the rest" (25).
33. Fletcher interview.
34. Author's notes from a visit to the poolside, August 9, 2011.
35. Perspective on booking Season 37 is largely from Lickona interview, 2011.
36. Ed Bailey, interview with the author, September 20, 2006, Austin; cassette recording. He refers to Texas artists, including the beloved late blues guitarist Stevie Ray Vaughan and Lyle Lovett, as well as Austin groups who gained popularity since 2000.
37. Ibid.
38. Ibid.
39. Ibid.
40. Lickona interview, 2007.

Chapter 10

1. Ray Lucero, interview with the author, August 9, 2011, Austin; digital recording.
2. Clifford Endres, *Austin City Limits* (Austin: University of Texas Press, 1987), 42.
3. John T. Davis, *Austin City Limits: 25 Years of American Music* (New York: Billboard Books, 2000), 85. Lickona wrote the account printed in Davis's book, which is the source for this paragraph's remaining details about booking Domino.
4. On the recording and the festival invitation, see Jon Pareles, "Fats Domino Sets an Example for New Orleans," *New York Times*, February 28, 2006, accessed January 15, 2013; http://www.nytimes.com/2006/02/28/arts/28fats.html?_r=0. Domino's health ultimately prevented his performance from taking place. On the replacement of the Medal, originally presented in 1998 by President Clinton, see the National Endowment for the Arts website, accessed January 15, 2013; http://arts.gov/NEARTS/2006v5-after-disaster-reclaiming-culture-gulf-coast/national-medal-arts-lost-hurricanes.
5. Michael Toland, interview with the author, August 10, 2011, Austin; digital recording.
6. Toland interview. The Rock and Roll Hall of Fame is the repository for this material.
7. Toland interview. The company Media Recall was doing the project at the time we spoke.
8. In cases where the DVD releases show the entire performance rather than the original broadcast edit, audio engineers at New West remix some of the sound, altering it in some cases from the original.

9. Ed Bailey, interview with the author, September 20, 2006, Austin; cassette recording.

10. Colin Pope, "Journal Profile—Tom Gimbel, General Manager, Austin City Limits," *Austin Business Journal* (April 8, 2011), accessed November 10, 2013; http://www.bizjournals.com/austin/print-edition/2011/04/08/journal-profile---tom-gimbel.html.

11. Ed Bailey, interview with the author, July 7, 2010, Austin; digital recording.

12. Terry Lickona, interview with the author, August 11, 2011, Austin; digital recording.

13. Marketing plan for this idea from the company Edges, Inc., is found in a proposal dated November 11, 1998; document located in the "cage" material at station KLRU, since relocated to the Rock and Roll Hall of Fame in Cleveland.

14. Lickona interview, 2011.

15. Ibid.

16. Ibid.

17. Terry Lickona, interview with the author, July 9, 2007, Austin; digital recording. During the interview, Lickona misspoke and said "twenty years"; I corrected it since he clearly meant "thirty years."

18. Lickona interview, 2007.

Postlude

1. The period is indeed part of the band's name.

2. Terry Lickona, personal communication, November 4, 2013.

BIBLIOGRAPHY

Books and Monographs:

Black, Louis, Doug Freeman, and Austin Powell. *The Austin Chronicle Music Anthology.* Austin: University of Texas Press, 2011. eBook Collection (EBSCOhost), EBSCOhost (accessed December 12, 2012).

Bourdieu, Pierre. *Distinction: A Social Critique of the Judgement of Taste.* Translated by Richard Nice. Cambridge, MA: Harvard University Press, 1984.

———. *The Field of Cultural Production: Essays on Art and Literature,* edited by Randal Johnson. New York: Columbia University Press, 1993.

———. *On Television.* Translated by Priscilla Parkhurst Ferguson. New York: The New Press, 1998.

Caldwell, John T. *Televisuality: Style, Crisis, and Authority in American Television.* New Brunswick, NJ: Rutgers University Press, 1995.

Creeber, Glen, ed. *The Television Genre Book.* London: British Film Institute, 2001.

Davis, John T. *Austin City Limits: 25 Years of American Music.* New York: Billboard Books, 2000.

Day, James. *The Vanishing Vision: The Inside Story of Public Television.* Berkeley: University of California Press, 1995. Accessed October 18, 2012. http://publishing.cdlib.org/ucpressebooks/view?docId=ft7x0nb54q&chunk.id=d0e36&toc.id=&toc.depth=1&brand=ucpress&anchor.id=bkd0e84#X.

Endres, Clifford. *Austin City Limits.* Austin: The University of Texas Press, 1987.

Farley, Jeffrey Ellrick. "Culture Industry as Cottage Industry: The Production of Musical Meaning in Austin, Texas." PhD dissertation, The University of Texas, 1996.

Herron, Edward A. *Miracle of the Air Waves: A History of Radio.* New York: Julian Messner, 1969.

Holt, Fabian. *Genre in Popular Music*. Chicago: University of Chicago Press, 2007.

Ishikawa, Sakae, ed. *Quality Assessment of Television*. Luton, Bedfordshire, UK: University of Luton Press, 1996.

Johnson, Julian. *Who Needs Classical Music? Cultural Choice and Musical Value*. New York: Oxford University Press, 2002.

Kahn, Frank J., ed. *Documents of American Broadcasting*, 4th ed. Englewood Cliffs, NJ: Prentice-Hall, 1984.

Lakoff, George. *Women, Fire, and Dangerous Things: What Categories Reveal About the Mind*. Chicago: University of Chicago Press, 1987.

Lena, Jennifer C. *Banding Together: How Communities Create Genres in Popular Music*. Princeton, NY: Princeton University Press, 2012.

Lickona, Terry, and Scott Newton, eds. *Austin City Limits: 35 Years in Photographs*. Austin: University of Texas Press, 2010.

Long, Joshua. *Weird City: Sense of Place and Creative Resistance in Austin, Texas*. Austin: University of Texas Press, 2010.

MacCannell, Dean. *The Tourist: A New Theory of the Leisure Class*. New York: Schocken Books, 1976.

Malone, Bill. *Country Music, U.S.A.* rev. ed. Austin: University of Texas Press, 1985.

Middleton, Richard. *Studying Popular Music*. Milton Keynes, Buckinghamshire, UK: Open University Press, 1990.

Mundy, John. *Popular Music on Screen: From Hollywood Musical to Music Video*. Manchester: Manchester University Press, 1999.

Nelson, Willie, with Bud Shrake. *Willie: An Autobiography*. New York: Simon and Schuster, 1988.

O'Connor, Alan, ed. *Raymond Williams on Television: Selected Writings*. London: Routledge, 1989.

Ouellette, Laurie. *Viewers Like You? How Public TV Failed the People*. New York: Columbia University Press, 2002.

Patoski, Joe Nick. *Willie Nelson: An Epic Life*. New York: Little, Brown and Company, 2008.

Peterson, Richard A., and Andy Bennett, eds. *Music Scenes: Local, Translocal, and Virtual*. Nashville: Vanderbilt University Press, 2004.

Raboy, Marc, ed., *Public Broadcasting for the 21st Century*. London: University of Luton Press, 1995.

Sconce, Jeffrey. *Haunted Media: Electronic Presence from Telegraphy to Television*. Durham, NC: Duke University Press, 2000.

Shank, Barry. *Dissonant Identities: The Rock and Roll Scene in Austin, Texas*. Hanover, NH: University Press of New England, 1994.

Smith, Chris. *101 Albums That Changed Popular Music*. New York: Oxford University Press, 2009.

Sparks, Hugh Cullen. "The Stylistic Development and Compositional Processes of Selected Solo Singer/Songwriters in Austin, Texas." PhD dissertation, University of Texas, 1984.

Spigel, Lynn, and Jan Olsson, eds. *Television After TV: Essays on a Medium in Transition.* Durham: Duke University Press, 2004.

Stimeling, Travis. *Cosmic Cowboys and New Hicks: The Countercultural Sounds of Austin's Progressive Country Music Scene.* New York: Oxford University Press, 2011.

Thompson, Todd M. "A Sound Divided: The Battles of Musical Space in Austin, Texas." MA thesis, University of Texas, 2010.

Thornton, Sarah. *Club Cultures: Music, Media, and Subcultural Capital.* Hanover, NH: University Press of New England, 1996.

Tracey, Michael. *The Decline and Fall of Public Service Broadcasting.* New York: Oxford University Press, 1998.

Interviews by the Author

Arhos, Bill. July 12, 2007. Austin, Texas. Digital recording.

Bailey, Ed. September 20, 2006. Austin. Cassette recording.

———. September 25, 2009. Telephone conversation.

———. July 7, 2010. Austin. Digital recording.

Benson, Ray. July 6, 2010. Austin. Digital recording.

Fletcher, Freddy. With Tim Neece. July 8, 2010. Austin. Digital recording.

Hickey, Lisa. July 8, 2010. Austin. Digital recording.

Hough, David. July 12, 2007. Austin. Digital recording.

Jones, Charlie. July 8, 2010. Austin. Digital recording.

Lickona, Terry. September 20, 2006. Austin. Cassette recording.

———. July 9, 2007. Austin. Digital recording.

———. July 6, 2010. Austin. Digital recording.

———. August 11, 2011. Austin. Digital recording.

Lucero, Ray. August 9, 2011. Austin. Digital recording.

Menotti, Gary. July 7, 2010. Austin. Digital recording.

———. Conversation with Doug Robb. July 10, 2007. Austin. Digital recording.

Moorhead, Robert. July 13, 2007. Austin. Digital recording.

Neece, Tim. With Freddy Fletcher. July 8, 2010. Austin. Digital recording.

Newton, Scott. July 13, 2007. Austin. Digital recording.

Olden, Walter. July 13, 2007. Austin. Digital recording.

Peterson, Jeff. July 13, 2007. Austin. Digital recording.

Robb, Doug. July 10, 2007. Austin. Digital recording.

Sullivan, Maury. August 10, 2011. Austin. Digital recording.

Toland, Michael. August 10, 2011. Austin. Digital recording.

Interviews by Others

NOTE: All below are part of the Austin City Limits Oral History Project Records, 2007, Dolph Briscoe Center for American History, The University of Texas at Austin; interviews took place in Austin and DVD copies in author's files unless otherwise noted.

Benson, Ray. By Stephanie Brown. April 5, 2007.
Nichols, Leslie. By Emily Wilkinson. April 11, 2007.
Scafe, Bruce. Telephone interview by Talor Schaddalee, April 20, 2007. Digital audio recording.
Wilson, Eddie. By Thomas Fawcett and Jazmin Cavazos. April 12, 2007.

Journal Articles and Book Chapters

Albers, Robert. "Quality in Television From the Perspective of the Professional Programme Maker." In *Quality Assessment of Television*, edited by Sakae Ishikawa, 101–44. Luton, Bedfordshire, UK: University of Luton Press, 1996.
Anderson, Carolyn. "Contested Public Memories: Hawaiian History as Hawaiian or American Experience." In *Television Histories: Shaping Collective Memory in the Media Age*, edited by Gary R. Edgerton and Peter C. Rollins, 143–68. Lexington: University Press of Kentucky, 2001.
Bay-Cheng, Sarah. "Theater Is Media: Some Principles for a Digital Historiography of Performance." *Theater* 42, no. 2 (2012): 26–41.
Benjamin, Walter. "The Work of Art in the Age of Mechanical Reproduction." In *Art in Modern Culture: An Anthology of Critical Texts*, edited by Francis Frascina and Jonathan Harris, 297–307. London: Phaidon Press Limited, 1992.
Benson, Michaela. "Living the 'Real' Dream in *la France profonde*? Lifestyle Migration, Social Distinction, and the Authenticities of Everyday Life." *Anthropological Quarterly* 86, no. 2 (Spring 2013): 501–25.
Berger, Arthur Asa. "Tourism as a Postmodern Semiotic Activity." *Semiotica* 183, no. 4 (2011): 105–19. Accessed October 12, 2013. doi: 10.1515/semi.2011.006.
Ferejohn, John A., and Roger G. Noll. "An Experimental Market for Public Goods: The PBS Station Program Cooperative." *The American Economic Review* 66, no. 2 (May 1976): 267–73.
Feuer, Jane. "The Concept of Live Television: Ontology as Ideology." In *Regarding Television: Critical Approaches—An Anthology*, edited by E. Ann Kaplan, 12–22. Frederick, MD: University Publications of America, 1983).
Forman, Murray. "'One night on TV is worth weeks at the Paramount': Musicians and Opportunity in Early Television, 1948–55." *Popular Music* 21, no. 3 (2002): 249–76.
Forristal, Linda Joyce, Dawn Gay Marsh, and Xinran Y. Lehto. "Revisiting MacCannell's Site Sacralization Theory as an Analytical Tool: Historic

Prophetstown as a Case Study." *International Journal of Tourism Research* 13 (2011): 570–82. Accessed October 10, 2013. doi: 10.1002/jtr.830.

Green, Archie. "Austin's Cosmic Cowboys: Words in Collision." In *"And Other Neighborly Names": Social Process and Cultural Image in Texas Folklore*, edited by Richard Bauman and Roger D. Abrahams, 152–94. Austin: The University of Texas Press, 1981.

Heyer, Paul. "Live from the Met: Digital Broadcast Cinema, Medium Theory, and Opera for the Masses." *Canadian Journal of Communication* 33 (2008): 591–604.

Laing, Stuart. "Raymond Williams and the Cultural Analysis of Television." *Media, Culture and Society* 13 (1991): 153–69.

Lena, Jennifer C., and Richard A. Peterson. "Classification as Culture: Types and Trajectories of Music Genres." *American Sociological Review* 73 (2008): 697–718.

Mellard, Jason Dean. "Home With the Armadillo: Public Memory and Performance in the 1970s Austin Music Scene." *Journal of Texas Music History* 10, no. 1 (2010): 1–14. Accessed June 16, 2014. http://ecommons.txstate.edu/jtmh/vol10/iss1/3.

Miller, Karl Hagstrom. "That's Right, You're Not from Texas: Exploring Some Outside Influences on Texas Music." *The Journal of Texas Music History* 1, no. 2 (fall 2001): 5–16.

Negus, Keith. "Musicians on Television: Visible, Audible and Ignored." *Journal of the Royal Music Association* 131, Part 2 (2006): 310–30.

Peterson, Richard A. "The Unnatural History of Rock Festivals: An Instance of Media Facilitation." *Popular Music and Society* 2 (1976): 1–26.

Porcello, Thomas. "Music Mediated as Live in Austin: Sound, Technology, and Recording Practice." In *Wired for Sound: Engineering and Technologies in Sonic Cultures*, edited by Paul D. Greene and Thomas Porcello, 103–117. Middletown, CT: Wesleyan University Press, 2005.

Saffle, Michael. "Rural Music on American Television, 1948–2010." In *Music in Television: Channels of Listening*, edited by James Deaville, 81–101. London: Routledge, 2011.

Vianello, Robert. "The Power Politics of 'Live' Television." *Journal of Film and Video* 38 (summer 1985): 26–40.

Wade, Leslie A. "The London Theatre Goes Digital: Divergent Responses to the New Media." *Theatre Symposium* 19 (2011): 54–68.

Audio and Video Recordings

Friedman, Kinky. *Kinky Friedman: Live from Austin Texas.* Directed by Gary Menotti, 59 min. New West Records, B000RF1QNI, 2007.

Murphey, Michael Martin. *Cosmic Cowboy Souvenir.* Beverly Hills, CA: A&M, SP-4388, 1973.

Stevie Ray Vaughan and Double Trouble: Live from Austin, Texas. DVD. Epic Music Video, EVD 50130, 1989; 1995.

Texas Folk & Outlaw Music at the Kerrville Festival. Edsel Records/Adelphi Records, EDCD 352, 1983; 1992.

Newspapers and Magazines

N.a. "Music: Groover's Paradise." *Time*, September 9, 1974. Accessed April 22, 2011.http://www.time.com/time/magazine/article/0,9171,904125-2,00. html.

N.a. "Will Stations Leave 'Limits' Behind?" *Austin American-Statesman*, January 12, 1996.

Alterman, Lorraine. "Shine On Country Soul: Pop." *New York Times*, May 19, 1974.

Arar, Yardena. " 'Austin City Limits' Marks its 15th Year." *Laredo Morning Times*, January 25, 1990.

Black, Louis. "Page Two: Seasons Change, and So Do We." *Austin Chronicle*, October 6, 2006. Accessed April 10, 2013. http://www.austinchronicle. com/columns/2006-10-06/408182.

Buchholz, Brad. "Beyond the Cosmic Cowboys." *Dallas Morning News*, February 25, 1990.

Corcoran, Michael. "A Dynamic Duet for 'Austin City Limits.' " *Austin American-Statesman*, September 17, 2004.

———. " 'Austin City Limits' Festival Promoter Savors the Sweet Sound of Success." *Austin American-Statesman*, September 19, 2003.

Cusic, Don. "Neil Reshen: Riding Herd on the New Breed." *Record World*, March 6, 1976; 6, 34, 40–41, 45.

Davis, John T. "Austin City Limits." *Austin American-Statesman XLent*, January 12, 1995.

———. "Expanding the Borders of 'Austin City Limits.' " *Austin American-Statesman*, July 30, 1982.

Dinges, Gary. "Study: Austin's creative sector has $4.35 billion economic impact." *Austin American-Statesman*, March 12, 2012. Accessed May 2, 2013.http://www.statesman.com/news/business/study-austins-creative-sector-has-435-billion-ec-1/nRmBW/.

Endres, Clifford. "Redneck Music and Public TV." *American Way*, February 15, 1989: 52–60.

Evans, Rush. "Bob Wills and His Texas Playboys." *Discoveries*, 1998. Accessed June 28, 2010. http://www.texasplayboys.net/Biographies/bobwillsbio.htm.

Frolik, Joe. "Keeping in Tune with 'Austin City Limits.' " *Austin American-Statesman*, October 1, 1978.

Gibson, Gwen. "Stars Shine Bright in 'Austin City Limits.' " *Savannah Morning News*, August 22, 1994.

———. "Texas City Is 'Music to Your Ears.'" *Savannah Morning News*, August 21, 1994.

Gradziel, Marybeth. "Austin City Limits." *The Austin Chronicle*, March 25, 1988.

Halbersberg, Elianne. "Austin City Limits." *Mix* 33, no. 3 (March 2009): 30–32.

Holloway, Diane. "Upstaged? New PBS Series from NY Prompts Discussion of Future of Long-Running KLRU Staple 'Austin City Limits.'" *Austin American-Statesman*, June 28, 1997.

———. "Updated but Downsized." *Austin American-Statesman*, January 30, 1998.

Johnson, Steve. "Back to the Roots: Channel 11 Pays a Rare Visit to the Fine Musicians of 'Austin City Limits.'" *Chicago Tribune*, June 12, 1998. Accessed December 11, 2012.http://articles.chicagotribune.com/1998-06-12/ features/ 9806120393_1_austin-city-limits-robert-earl-keen-son-volt.

Lampert-Greaux, Ellen. "Beyond City Limits." *Live Design* 45, no. 6 (August 2011): 20–25.

McCleese, Don. "'ACL' Still Hasn't Reached Its Limits." *Austin American-Statesman*, January 14, 1993.

———. "A Mecca for Musical Mavericks." *Billboard* 110, no. 21, May 23, 1998. Accessed December 14, 2011. Business Source Complete.

McGee, David. "What Is Progressive Country?" *Record World*, March 6, 1976.

Nichols, Lee. "'ACL's' 16th Year Packs Momentum." *Austin American-Statesman* January 17, 1991.

Pallmeyer, Karl. "The Maestro in the Control Booth." *Austin Business Journal*, July 7–13, 1995.

Pareles, Jon. "'Austin City Limits:' Live Music, No Frills." *New York Times* 138, May 19, 1989. Accessed December 14, 2011. LexisNexis.

———. "Fats Domino Sets an Example for New Orleans." *New York Times*, February 28, 2006. Accessed January 15, 2013.http://www.nytimes.com/2006/02/28/arts/28fats.html?_r=0.

Perry, Claudia. "15 Years of 'Austin City Limits.'" *The Houston Post*, January 25, 1990.

Point, Michael. "Loud and Clear: 'Austin City Limits' Shows U.S. Variety of Music for 15 Years." *Austin American-Statesman*, January 19, 1990.

Ratliff, Ben. "Guitarist Clarence Gatemouth Brown Dies at 81." *New York Times*, September 12, 2005. Accessed August 21, 2012. http://www.nytimes.com/2005/09/12/arts/music/12brown.html?_r=1.

Reuters. "TV's Austin City Limits Branches Out but Retains Intimate Feel." *Reuters*, October 12, 2012. Accessed October May 14,2014.http://www.reuters.com/ article/2012/10/12/uk-usa-entertainment-austin-idUSLNE89B02020121012.

Rindy, Dean. "Country Karma." *The Texas Observer*, April 14, 1972.

St. John, Bob. "Willie Nelson—A Real Man." *Scene* (August 10, 1975): 13.

Slater, Wayne. "'Austin City Limits' Moves to Changing Beat." *Dallas Morning News*, February 10, 1985.

Steffans, Mildred. "The Case for Visualized Music in Television." *Telescreen: For the Arts of Television* (Spring 1945): 8–12.

Szilagyi, Pete. "KLRU Survives in Network World." *Austin American-Statesman*, September 2, 1990.

Werts, Diane. "How to Wow a Critic," *Newsday (Queens Edition)*, July 12, 1998.

Williams, Larry. "Willie Nelson Was Limit." *Memphis Commercial Appeal*, March 24, 1975.

Yardley, Jim. "Austin Journal; A Slogan Battle Keeps Austin Weird." *New York Times*, December 8, 2002. Accessed May 2, 2013. http://www.nytimes.com/2002/12/08/us/austin-journal-a-slogan-battle-keeps-austin-weird.html.

Collections

Barker Texas History Collection. Dolph Briscoe Center for American History. The University of Texas at Austin. Austin, Texas.

Bill Arhos Collection of *Austin City Limits*. Southwestern Writers Collection. The Wittliff Collections. Texas State University–San Marcos. San Marcos, Texas.

The "Cage." Archival materials collected in boxes at KLRU; since relocated to the Rock and Roll Hall of Fame in Cleveland, Ohio.

Country Music Foundation Archives. Country Music Hall of Fame® and Museum. Nashville, Tennessee.

Southern Folklife Collection. The Wilson Library. University of North Carolina at Chapel Hill. Chapel Hill, North Carolina.

Troupe Earnest Gammage Papers, 1981–1992. Dolph Briscoe Center for American History. The University of Texas at Austin. Austin, Texas.

Vertical Files. Dolph Briscoe Center for American History. The University of Texas at Austin. Austin, Texas.

INDEX